Dr. Gary S. Goodman

Selling Skills
for the
Nonsalesperson
For People Who Hate to Sell
But Love to Succeed

A SPECTRUM BOOK

Prentice-Hall, Inc., Englewood Cliffs, New Jersey 07632

Library of Congress Cataloging in Publication Data
Goodman, Gary S.
  Selling skills for the nonsalesperson.

  "A Spectrum Book."
  Includes index.
  1. Selling. I. Title.
HF5438.25.G66   1984   658.8'5   83-17675
ISBN 0-13-805961-6
ISBN 0-13-805953-5 (pbk.)

This book is available at a special discount when ordered
in bulk quantities. Contact Prentice-Hall, Inc., General
Publishing Division, Special Sales, Englewood Cliffs, N. J. 07632.

**This book is dedicated to
my wife and best friend, Dr. Deanne Honeyman-Goodman;
to the memory of my father, Bernard Goodman;
and to the memory of Roy Honeyman.**

© 1984 by Gary S. Goodman

A SPECTRUM BOOK

Editorial/production supervision: Suse L. Cioffi
Cover design: Hal Siegel
Manufacturing buyer: Patrick Mahoney

ISBN 0-13-805953-5 {PBK.}

ISBN 0-13-805961-6

3 4 5 6 7 8 9 10

Printed in the United States of America

Prentice-Hall International, Inc., *London*
Prentice-Hall of Australia Pty. Limited, *Sydney*
Prentice-Hall of Canada Inc., *Toronto*
Prentice-Hall of India Private Limited, *New Delhi*
Prentice-Hall of Japan, Inc., *Tokyo*
Prentice-Hall of Southeast Asia Pte. Ltd., *Singapore*
Whitehall Books Limited, *Wellington, New Zealand*
Editora Prentice-Hall do Brasil Ltda., *Rio de Janeiro*

Contents

Introduction   v

chapter one

The Selling Game   1

chapter two

How to Put Your Best *Self* Forward   26

chapter three

Profile of the Successful Salesperson   47

chapter four

Anatomy of a Sale   68

chapter five

Mastering Objections and Difficult Customers   99

chapter six
Professional Telemarketing Techniques   119

Afterword   134

Index   135

Introduction

If we were to take a census of the number of salespeople in America, the count would exceed 220 million, because *everyone is a salesperson*. Some people are simply better at it than the others who are less aware of the sales situations in which they find themselves.

Few things are as challenging or as misunderstood as the selling process. Selling is a means of bringing all of our personal resources to bear upon a single situation. While countless people are called upon each day to sell themselves, their ideas, as well as their products and services, most don't have the first idea as to how to do it.

This book is written for *nonsalespeople* as well as new salespeople. It is designed to show you the essentials of the sales process without the "insider-mumbo-jumbo" in manuals intended for people already in the sales field. After reading this book, you should know more about the selling game, the profile of a successful salesperson, how to handle yourself in-person and over the phone, and how to construct a winning sales presentation. You will also encounter the Customer Matrix, which is a new tool for determining which prospects are worthwhile and which ones you'll want to avoid. You'll also learn the *Goodman Method*™ for managing difficult people and resistance.

I hope you enjoy *Selling Skills for the Nonsalesperson* and find substantial benefit in it. If it helps you to feel more comfortable with selling, as well as better informed about it, I will feel I have been successful.

—Gary S. Goodman, Ph.D., Glendale, CA

chapter one

The selling game

I know, you're not a salesperson. You probably never wanted to be one, and, as a matter of fact, you don't even like them very much as a group. Furthermore, the idea of persuading somebody to do something by resorting to various tricks of the salesperson's trade is a real turn-off to you.

So, why are you reading this book? Oh, you were attracted by the title, because it promises to be different. This book seems like it's really for "normal people"—people who don't wear neon suits and plastic smiles.

It's true. This book *is* for you if you are one of many millions of regular people who are called upon to induce their fellow earthlings to do things they might otherwise not do, like get out and vote, give a few dollars to a worthy cause, keep appointments made with attorneys, doctors, and other busy people, and invest in purchases that will increase their happiness and well-being.

All of us, at one time or other, are called into an arena that resembles an old fashioned showdown. We have to stand face to face with a customer or business associate and draw upon our inner resources and skills to "get our own way." What happens to most of us when we're on the spot like this? We reach down for our sixgun and either can't pull the trigger, and actually formulate a persuasive message, or, perhaps worse still, we find our gun isn't loaded. We lack the skills to effectively move the other person to action, or change his or her attitudes about a particular matter.

For most of us, our problem isn't in the fact that we have never "sold" anything before. We're all salespeople, because in looking out for ourselves we have had to "sell" others on giving us job opportunities. We have also engineered cooperation from others to get along with the business of living from day to day. Our problem is in large measure attributable to the fact that we are *unconscious* salespeople instead of *conscious* ones. Once we begin to understand the need to heighten our awareness of the many selling situations we all encounter daily, we will be on the way to becoming more effective people.

SALESPEOPLE ARE NOT BORN

Contrary to popular belief, salespeople are not born with skills that the rest of us don't have. In fact, some of the very best salespeople had to force themselves to change their natural behavior patterns in order to develop a successful sales regimen. Others report that they had to master personal obstacles. It is truly amazing to discover how many great salespeople stuttered at one time in their lives. Still others had to overcome such terrible shyness that selling became a sort of compensatory therapy, through which they systematically un-learned how to be shy, and substituted an outgoing personality in its place.

Just as brain surgeons and great artists need to become refined through training, discipline, and controlled practice, salespeople need to perfect their raw talents to become real professionals.

THE IMAGE OF SALESPEOPLE IN AMERICA

From time to time, sociologists perform a national survey to determine the status of various occupations in America. At the top of the pecking order are supreme court justices, doctors, and other members of the classical professions. Almost invariably, in the lowest part of the scale one will find salespeople. Why are salespeople so poorly considered?

I asked a large group of seminar attendees at a prestigious company to brainstorm a list of associations they made with the word *salesperson*.

Some of their responses were: "unscrupulous;" "will do anything for a sale;" "liars;" "phony;" "abrasive;" and "insensitive." You could probably add a thought or two to this list, yourself.

I was somewhat surprised by the fact that nobody offered a positive term to describe salespeople. We most certainly could, couldn't we? How about: "friendly;" "outgoing;" "helpful;" "patient;" and the like? Truly *good* salespeople possess these qualities, and many more, as we will mention in a later section.

PEOPLE LOVE TO BUY, BUT HATE TO BE SOLD

An old adage well known to experienced salespeople is "People love to buy, but hate to be sold." This is a clever way of saying that people enjoy the benefits of consuming products and services, but it is important for them to think that they persuaded themselves instead of feeling they are the passive pawns of an overpowering or charismatic seller.

A part of this "I'll make my own decision" philosophy stems from our need to feel in control of our own faculties and financial resources, as well as from the good-old-American philosophy of self-sufficiency. The rapid rise of the supermarket concept over the last several decades demonstrates a desire on the part of people to set their own pace in shopping. Some would argue, though, that proprietors have gone too far in denying us access to clerks and salespeople who could quickly answer our questions and help us on our way.

SMASHING SOME SELLING MYTHS

Myth 1

The best salespeople are compulsive liars. It's true that a particular person can be induced to buy something based on the misrepresentations of an unscrupulous seller, but a business won't thrive and prosper if this is the typical treatment received by its patrons. Good businesses are built on satisfied customers, who not only make further purchases themselves, but encourage their friends and associates to do so as well.

In Los Angeles, there is a restaurant named, "Palermo." It's a nice, little spot with good food, reasonable prices, and perhaps most important, great people in charge. What is truly amazing about this place is the number of boosters it has created among its patrons. Management makes you feel at home right away with a complementary glass of wine or a soft drink. This kind of gesture usually is limited to the expensive places that are charging you for the same privilege through outrageous prices. Throughout the meal management shows concern for your satisfaction, and as you leave, you receive a robust word of thanks.

In short, the people at Palermo sell us on feeling good, and we love it. In fact, I am amazed at the number of people from different walks of life who ask me if I have been to Palermo because they think it's such a great place.

Myth 2

Salespeople must be abrasive to be effective. A number of folks believe that selling inevitably involves rubbing people the wrong way. Well, it's true that from a statistical standpoint, we aren't going to please everybody, and if we speak to enough people in order to be successful, we are bound to encounter some who out-and-out don't like us. This is one of the implications of the "Law Of Large Numbers," to which we will refer later.

Professional salespeople are very smooth, indeed. Much of their skill resides in the fact that the persuasion they use is not visible to the other person. The use of the skill is the equivalent of watching a brilliant magician at work. We are enchanted by the outcome, and even more boggled by the fact that we can't figure out the means through which the end was accomplished. Good salespeople, like good magicians, will also tend to make their work seem effortless, which increases the admiration of the observer even more.

I know a person who went into the insurance business not very long ago. The first thing he did, which insurance companies encourage for obvious reasons, was call upon his friends to buy. He called me on the phone and used a "canned pitch" that had been provided for him. Being somewhat of an expert in telephone selling, I was painfully aware of the techniques that were being used on me. Frankly, I resented them, although I liked my friend very much.

What is the moral to this story? It's this: Any technique that brings too much attention to itself, and diverts the customer's attention from the item being sold, will cause the selling effort to fail. Abrasiveness on the part of a salesperson may be seen as a *technique*, in this sense.

At the same time, if a salesperson seems to rely too much on any sort of gimmick, the sale will probably fall through. Gushiness or an overly effusive manner will be a turn-off to many, just as a sour face can chill yet others.

Myth 3

Deep down, salespeople feel terrible about what they are doing for a living, and if they could, they would get out of that line of work. Ask a salesperson who is successful the following question: "What is the best job in the world?" Do you know what the answer will be? "Mine."

That's right, salespeople are sold on their means of making a living, because in selling they have a way of attaining an entire constellation of personal and professional goals. Selling is one of the only occupations in America in which one's earnings are limited only by one's own drive and abilities. If you sell more, you make more.

Think about the number of times that you may have had the following thoughts.

> I don't know what it is about John. He never pulls his weight, and yet he gets the same paycheck that I do. I wish he'd get with it, or management would let him know he's demoralizing the rest of us.

This scenario is played out day after day across the country. The complainer usually fails to see that there are only two ways to break out of a cycle of unfairness and despair, such as that brought on by equal pay for *unequal* work. One method of liberation is starting your own business while promising yourself that you will never create the injustices that you have suffered at the hands of other bosses and organizations. For many, this dream of independence will remain only a dream.

The more practical alternative is to get into sales, where there is an attempt to reward performance with the right amount of pay. In one sense, the purest compensation plan in industry today is what is referred to as a *straight commission* structure. In a nutshell, it says: If you produce, you get paid; and, if you don't, you don't earn anything.

This pay plan, though it isn't for everybody, is the closest thing we will ever get to perfect justice in terms of compensation. Through it, we are told, produce a lot, and earn a lot. I know a person in pharmaceutical and hospital sales who has grown rich over the years from his sales production. He claims he wouldn't ever want to work on anything other than a straight commission plan, while pointing out that if it hadn't been for this structure, he wouldn't have been able to grow wealthy through his labors.

Myth 4

Selling isn't fun. People who convince themselves that selling involves unrelenting drudgery aren't seeing the potential for quality in the job. Most of the salespeople I come into contact with are as fun-loving as one can get, and they insist on making their work reflect their spirit, even if they are dealing with a dull prospects.

Much of the fun in the job is derived from the feeling that the outcome of every working day isn't neatly predetermined, as it is in so many walks of life. When salespeople make phone calls or a personal visits, they could be walking into a commercial paradise or veritable bear-trap. Now, that's exciting, and for the stout of heart, exhilarating!

Myth 5

Selling is exhausting and personally overwhelming. It's true that if you care about what you are doing, you will exert a lot of energy in pursuit of your goal. This applies to salespeople, as well.

A funny thing happens to salespeople though, just as it does to athletes who find themselves in an exciting contest. Just when they feel they don't have any more to give, they dig down deeper inside, and find that they have more energy to expend. If they are successful and they "win," they often find that their energies are revived to such a point that they don't want to wind down.

Selling only becomes personally overwhelming when the salesperson is unskilled or when he or she brings an improper attitude to the challenge.

MASTERING THE PERSONAL PSYCHOLOGY OF SELLING

Selling isn't so complex an art that it is incapable of being taught or learned. Like any set of procedures, selling is something that can be cultivated through selective exposure and repetition of learned responses.

The reason most people don't do well in selling is because they defeat themselves psychologically by being unprepared for the demands placed upon them to respond effectively to various events.

Here are some of the psychological hurdles that the non-salesperson will have to surpass:

Rejection and the Fear of Rejection

It's probably fair to say that almost all of us love to be accepted and welcomed by others. Our need to affiliate is well documented by anthropologists and other social scientists. When we are denied the approval of others, we often grow alienated and psychologically unbalanced.

We exaggerate our need for acceptance, however, to such a point that this perceived need becomes debilitating. Rather than manage the inevitable rebuffs and rejections that occur from time to time, we overreact and become deeply disturbed whenever anyone withholds his or her approval.

This unsettling state is so uncomfortable that we find ourselves avoiding situations in which we find ourselves subjected to rejection. By doing so, we are, at the very same time, denying ourselves the prospect of improving our situation. As Bette Davis said, "No guts—no glory."

At the bottom of our exaggerated concern to avoid rejection probably is the endorsement of what some psychologists would call a *false belief*. This belief is something we have told ourselves that acts to keep us from responding intelligently and rationally in various situations. For instance, we may have told ourselves, "Its *awful* whenever anybody rejects me, and I will avoid this horrible state at all costs."

What we need to do is actively dispute the wisdom of this premise that rejection is somehow *necessarily* awful. Who said so, besides ourselves? Where is it written that rejection *has to be* awful? Why can't it simply be "mildly unsettling," or even, "amusing?"

There is nothing *inherent* in rejection that must debilitate us. In fact, I know some salespeople who very successfully divorce their egos from the act of rejection. They contend, and quite accurately, that prospects aren't rejecting *them*, but simply the sales message. They don't see any need to take the event personally.

Successful salespeople understand the *Law Of Large Numbers*. This law states that if you attempt an outcome a large number of times, the percentages for succeeding will be in your favor, and you are bound to succeed a number of times. Another way of seeing it, on the down side of course, is that you will have to properly manage the times in which you fail, as well.

PERFECTIONISM

Associated with the fear of rejection is *perfectionism*. As applied to sales, this means the nonsalesperson will probably be encumbered by a need to be "right" in all situations and will find trying to sell the "wrong" person, or one who will not say yes, as being very uncomfortable.

I have found that people with clerical backgrounds are riddled with perfectionism to such a extent that they would rather avoid making one small error than make a dozen lucrative sales. It's not only alright to be wrong, but it sometimes pays to admit small errors in front of prospects so they can fulfill their overwhelming need to be right.

Alexander King, in one of his autobiographical books, tells a story about the foolishness involved in perfectionism. He was working as a commercial artist on a particular account and was commissioned to draw an advertisement. He drew a flawless product and brought it into the client for his approval. The client stared at the work for several minutes, and then announced, "There's something wrong with it, but I don't know what it is."

King was astonished by the client's obvious lack of taste. He pondered the situation and finally determined that the client had an overbearing need to participate in the drawing in some way. The client's way of doing so was to criticize the product, even if it was flawless. King understood the man's need to be right, and rather than fight it, he introduced a minor but obvious flaw into the work and returned to the client's office for his opinion.

The client looked at the drawing, pointed out the newly introduced flaw, and said, "Change this one thing, here, and it will be fine." King made the repair, and the client ended up "buying" the exact piece that he had earlier rejected!

Perfectionism is problematic in other ways, as well. It is closely linked to procrastination. If we insist circumstances be perfect before undertaking a project, we will, in all likelihood, never get the thing underway.

FEAR OF FAILURE

I think the two words I heard more from my parents when growing up than any others were, "be careful." This was sage advice in a hostile world filled with speeding cars, hot stoves, and potentially bruising bumps. If a little child wasn't careful, he or she could really get hurt.

Most of us were warned about such hazards, and as we are still around to read these words, something must have sunk in. Unfortunately, along the way, something else crept into our consciousness—timidity and fear of failure.

We were told that failure was the worst thing in the world. In fact, the grading system in most communities placed an "F" grade at the bottom of the scale. If we didn't want to be stigmatized for life, we were warned, we should avoid that "F" at all costs.

In becoming paranoid about failing, we were unwittingly reducing our exposure to risk, as well. Risk is necessary to growth as human beings and as productive people. If we don't risk, we don't grow.

Salespeople are at risk constantly. Their egos are on the line with every encounter. They understand failure sufficiently to know that it sometimes precedes success, and at other times, accompanies it.

Thomas Edison performed some 2,000 experiments before he discovered the laws governing electricity. Someone reportedly walked up to him one day and asked, "How could you stand failing so many times?" His reply was, "I didn't fail. I simply discovered some 2,000 ways that electricity *didn't* work."

The great Babe Ruth is remembered for his prolific number of home runs, rather than for holding, at the same time, the distinction of having more strikeouts recorded against him than any other ballplayer of his era.

Lincoln is also memorialized for his contributions as President. The fact that he lost every single election before running for the Presidency is an obscure fact that few people would consider significant.

Salespeople are rewarded for their successes, and not for their failures. I have yet to encounter a pay plan that rewards salespeople for the proportion of "yesses" they produce relative to the number of prospects they see. People are paid for results, not for mere percentages that would be of greater interest to a statistician than to a businessperson.

FEAR OF SUCCESS

Why would anyone be afraid of succeeding? Wouldn't they be able to find places to spend their money?

Seriously, though, there are folks who would rather fail or stay where they are, instead of becoming phenomenal successes. Why is this so?

Fear of success, according to a number of psychologists, is really fear of *future failure*. People who succeed today, may experience a relapse tomorrow, when a lot more is expected of them. Rather than face the discomfort of a big failure, these people will not bother to be successful to begin with.

Some people believe they aren't worthy enough to deserve great success. They suffer from the guilt of some past deed or deeds, or their self-esteem has been thwarted by some other cause. So, their continuing failure is really a psychological atonement for their feelings of inadequacy.

Sometimes this sense of guilt is disguised as empathy for sales prospects. The salesperson asks him or herself, "How can I ask this person to buy such and such? Who am I to do this?" The salesperson answers his or her own question by saying, "I'm no good at running my own life, let alone making suggestions for others."

MONEY MYTHS

People are afraid of making money, or so it would seem to a visitor from another planet who looked at some of our superstitions about this medium of exchange.

If I asked you to fill in the following sentence, what words would you use?

Money is _____.

Try this one.

Money causes _____.

This one is a real winner.

Rich people are _____.

What did you put in the spaces? Money is "wonderful?" Money causes "us to feel free and happy?" Rich people are "having a ball?"

A number of folks would instead use some of the aphorisms and adages common in our culture. "Money is the root of all evil," is one oft-spoken line, as is, "Money causes unhappiness." Rich people are often accused of being "miserable."

I like to recall the movie, "Arthur," in which the rich aunt says something to the effect: "People are always saying that rich people are unhappy. I'm rich, and I've never had an unhappy day in my life!"

How many times have you heard people claim, "I only need enough money to get by on?" The same people will argue for the proposition that if they only had about 10 percent more than they are presently making, they'd be on easy street.

Here's another myth.

To get to the top you have to _____ along the way.

We could easily and accurately insert the words, "cooperate with a lot of people," and that would make sense. Most folks would automatically insert the words, "step on a lot of people," because this is what they have heard is the price one pays for success.

Myths such as these cause people to be ambivalent about being successful and about truly setting themselves apart as achievers. There is no necessary correlation between success and *un*happiness. Indeed, a compelling argument could be made for the proposition that it is the *unsuccessful* people in the world who cause others so many problems. The successful individuals are the ones who create surpluses, that can in turn be used in charitable as well as self-interested ways to create nicer products and job opportunities for the rest of us.

Perhaps the most devastating money myth to which we subscribe is contained in the notions "I can only make X amount of money," or "I can only sell somebody something after having built a long relationship with the person."

I once was featured before the Jonathan Club in Los Angeles as a speaker. My subject included references to the fact that we can accomplish a great deal by telephone, if we simply allow ourselves to do so. A few days later, I received a call from someone who heard the talk. He returned to his office after hearing the speech, and while speaking to a prospect who was considering the purchase of a computer the fellow decided to "go for the gusto," and ask for the okay on the phone, instead of waiting for the prospect to respond to literature and a personal visit. To his amazement, the prospect agreed to buy right on the phone.

The fellow was amazed at his accomplishment because somewhere, somebody said that a sale had to be orchestrated through a series of elaborate and traditional steps. Believing this, and never hearing it disputed, the fellow had lost countless opportunities to be of service because he was burdened with a false belief.

We need to liberate ourselves from the constraints of various fictions, especially when they come in the form of money myths.

OBSTACLES TO PEAK PERFORMANCE

A terrific little article appeared in *Esquire* magazine a while ago, entitled "How To Do It." The first line is a classic, I think. "First clear off enough space. Then make sure you have enough time." The remainder of the piece discusses how the reader can better accomplish anything.

I don't know how many times I have had to complete an important project, only to look at a cluttered desk, and almost be turned-off to the prospect of getting started. When this happens, I simply remember the *Esquire* article, and I begin by clearing away obstacles that could stand in my way without my being aware of them. Effective salespeople need to become aware of obstacles that are before them, as well, and many of them are subtle.

THE SECONDARY-GAIN TRAP

When I was leading a seminar in Amarillo, Texas a few years ago, I remember having an interesting exchange with a fellow who sold insurance. He seemed to have some pretty hard-and-fast ideas about selling, and I decided that it was important to hear some of these before trying to replace them with any of my own.

As I tried to illustrate a point, I noticed that he started frowning in disagreement. I stopped midway through the idea and asked, "Bill, how do you feel about that?"

Slowly, he looked up from his folded hands and said, "I'll tell you this: I don't care what you say; I won't sell anybody 'till they are my friend, first."

This seemed to be a curious obstacle that he was placing between himself and selling. I asked, "Do you mean that you will *only* sell friends of yours, and nobody else?"

"I'll sell others, too," he continued, "but I have to feel that I can sit down and talk with them about things that have nothing to do with insurance. Then I feel it is right to go ahead and make them a client."

I asked Bill if he was aware of the fact that he was probably turning down business from people who would be happy to be clients but who had no need to become friendlier. He said he was prepared to accept that outcome, because his personal code allowed him only to sell friends.

I have to admit that this seems like a peculiar idiosyncracy, on its surface. It isn't that strange, though. This fellow was falling into what is called the *secondary gain trap*. What he was doing was looking for *friendship*, when he should have been looking *for sales*. He had confused himself into believing that the most important determinant of sales was friendship, when this isn't the case with a number of prospects who are really indifferent to the idea of chatting with a salesperson on a topic other than that which pertains to their immediate insurance needs.

The secondary gain trap is often working in salespeople who are looking to avoid rejection, instead of looking to sell prospects. I know a number of companies that unknowingly encourage their sales staffers in this area by supplying them with brochures that can be sent out at the request of a prospect. I recognize that brochures are a way of life in business, but often they are used as an excuse to avoid commitment. When salespeople speak on the phone to prospects and are about to ask for the order, the buyer often will request a brochure. Instead of trying to close the deal at that moment, typical salespeople avoid the possibility of being rejected by consenting to mail a brochure, and by telling themselves that the brochure will do the selling. They then act surprised when they never hear from the prospect again.

I have actually formulated an answer to requests for brochures, that I suggest some of my clients use. "With all respect, Mr. Jones, we aren't in the brochure business, and in any case, brochures don't make decisions— people do. That's why we say, let's get started now, and see what you think, okay?"

You'll really know whether you have any reason to pursue a relationship with the prospect based upon the reaction he or she gives to this line.

LACK OF SELF-CONFIDENCE

Franklin Roosevelt said it best in, "We have nothing to fear, but fear, itself." The things that really concern us are not nearly as formidable as we think. Obstacles are made worse by our negative perception of them.

Successful salespeople aren't fearless. They learn to channel their fears constructively, so they build themselves up, instead of tear themselves down.

Confidence is learned, also. We aren't born with self-confidence, but build it up over time. One of the best ways to build self-confidence is to find out what you fear most, and then set out to overcome these obstacles, one by one.

Make a list of the things you fear most when it comes to selling. Do you fear rejection? Mark it down. Are you afraid of meeting people? Put that down, too. Are you afraid your product or service will be criticized by prospects? Note that, also.

Now develop some explicit exercises that *require you boldly move toward the things you fear most*. For instance, if you fear rejection, the best thing to do is work out a routine whereby you encounter the prospect of being rejected with great frequency. If you sell by knocking on doors, then knock on twice as many tomorrow as you did today. Observe what happens. Instead of finding the rejection you encounter doubly bad, you will find that you start to grow *insensitive* to it. Each instance of rejection begins to take on less importance. Your attitude becomes more resilient. Instead of pausing between presentations, you'll probably bounce back that much faster, after you have started to see more people.

Your odds of succeeding will improve, too. The more people you talk to, the greater are your chances of succeeding. Show me a good salesperson, and I'll show you someone who has self-confidence.

The best tonic for fear and a lack of self-confidence is *action*. When designing sales training programs for organizations, I try to get new recruits into action with customers as quickly as possible. Many companies make the mistake of investing small fortunes in product training before they give sales trainees a chance to do any selling. What this does is increase the fear of the trainee, unnecessarily. For example, if it takes two weeks to put a trainee into the field instead of six, the novice is going to be much less fearful because he will have had less time to worry about the job to be done, and the potential for failure.

Self-confidence can also be developed by remembering all of the times you were afraid of doing something, only to find that your fears were unfounded. Think of the many stressful situations that you have overcome in your life. You made it then, and you'll make it now, if you don't defeat yourself with self-doubts.

Many of the world's greatest performers report that they experience pangs of fear and a lack of confidence before undertaking important tasks. World-class actors and athletes speak of the butterflies that they get in the pit of their stomachs as an important event draws near. They come through beautifully, though, because they tell themselves that they are going to be successful, and a moment arrives when they put their fears behind them.

BUILDING SELF-ESTEEM

I tell every salesperson I meet that there is one thought that he or she has to believe to be successful: "I know what is good for the other person." If salespeople can't endorse this simple statement, they cannot be really successful. To be able to say this, we also need to hold ourselves in high regard.

Most of us defeat ourselves by telling ourselves that we don't amount to very much. We feed ourselves negative messages like, "I feel lousy," and "I'll never get my way," and "Who am I to tell this person what is good for him?"

Instead of these types of defeatist ideas, we should be giving ourselves *success messages*. Here are some of the things we should be telling ourselves.

> "I'm important."
> "I know what I'm talking about."
> "I'm going to really help this customer."
> "I'm going to get this sale."
> "I have the greatest product/service in the world."
> "This person will be glad he bought from me."
> "Life is wonderful."
> "Thank goodness I have my faculties, and I can change my life at any time by selling something and meeting new people."
> "The future holds great things in store for me."
> "Every contract with another person is a learning experience."

To keep your high regard for yourself, you should avoid people who are going to be *downers*. Complainers can get us so wrapped up in their discolored view of the world, that we become morose and depressed, as well. When you deal with a complainer, ask, "What's the *good* word, Bob?" This will either shut him or her up, or get him or her thinking on the right track.

We all know that in recent years the American economy has been troubled. Poor economic times have gotten a lot of people down, including a close friend of mine. I used to visit him and be cheerful, although I was finding business a little tough at the time. He would launch into his Chicken Little forecast about the great depression in which the world was falling. This negative attitude was strange coming from him. He used to inspire me through his toughness and self-reliant attitudes. I would listen to a little bit of his complaining and find I could tolerate no more. I'd say, "You know, friend, great fortunes are made in the worst of times." I then told him about plans for expanding my company smack in the middle of uncertain times. He didn't want to hear my optimism, so I decided not to deal with him. I didn't need anyone bringing me down with feelings of inadequacy. I am pleased to say that he later seemed to pull himself out of his personal depression, and he started to regain his confidence in himself and the economy.

NONTRADITIONAL SELLING

I spend a good deal of time in restaurants. I believe I have become an unofficial expert in restaurant marketing as a result.

Some restaurants are adept at making guests feel comfortable and important, while others remind me of a cattle call. Restaurants, whether they think so or not, are sales organizations. Like any business, they have as their first purpose the creation and retention of a customer. You will find that the most successful restaurants conduct their business as refined sales presentations. They literally sell us on eating certain meals, sell us on our enjoyment of them, and then sell us on returning again. An excellent example of a restaurant chain that employs sophisticated selling techniques is the Original Bobby McGee's Conglomeration of Arizona, California, and Hawaii.

Case Study: The Original Bobby McGee's Conglomeration

The reason my wife and I went to Bobby McGee's in Honolulu was because we were staying in the hotel that housed the restaurant. At first, we found it difficult to get a reservation, although the place was located a little bit off the beaten path. After a few days, we figured out that the trick was to reserve our table the evening before we decided to go. We got a six-thirty reservation, and when we arrived, we found a very unique operation.

The first thing we noticed was the Victorian decor, with interesting lamps, overstuffed furniture, and the like. In the middle of the restaurant was an old-fashioned bathtub that housed the salad bar. Adjoining the restaurant was a disco that hadn't started playing music upon our arrival.

We were invited to wait for our table either in the reception area or in the disco, where we could order a cocktail. When our table was ready, we were introduced to the restaurant by a fellow who was dressed in a Jolly Green Giant outfit. He introduced himself as the Jolly Green Midget, which told us that the evening wasn't going to be dull. The cocktail waitress came by within two minutes to take our order. She was dressed in a very revealing Robin Hood outfit. Sherwood Forest never looked like that before!

While we were deciding on cocktails, we noticed that the waiter attending the next table was dressed like a superhero, on the order of Superman or Batman. His enthusiasm was extraordinary. He carried a stick in his right hand that had a little plastic shark jaw on the end of it, which he would open and close by pulling a string. He retrieved his menus by having "Jaws," as he called his device, seize them from customers, who found the experience very funny.

There were two menus from which we could order. Because we arrived rather early in the evening, we could order from the early bird menu, which had reduced prices and limited offerings, or we could order from the regular one. We both chose an early bird meal and when the waiter took our order, he tried to gently talk us out of it, because he felt that the regular dinners were "a better value." Actually, the regular dinners were double the early bird prices. We stuck to our guns.

We noticed that all of the restaurant employees were wearing bizarre outfits. I noticed harem-girls, saloon girls, and guys dressed in tightly-fitted outfits that emphasized their physiques. This was a very sexually charged environment. It seemed constructed on some kind of behavioral principle that encouraged patrons to loosen-up and abandon the constraints that usually accompany us when we go out for dinner.

Every ten or fifteen minutes, a new face (and fantasy) would stop by our table and see how we were doing, and whether we wanted another drink. It seemed that if Robin Hood couldn't weaken one's resolve to not have another drink, Mata Hari could.

Soon after dinner arrived, the Green Midget asked us how it was, and if he could bring us anything else. Because we didn't order from the regular menu, he seemed to be rushing our table. He overpoured our water, and seemed to hover near us. As we were finishing the last few bites, he inquired as to whether we would like him to reserve us a table in the disco. We declined.

As we left the restaurant, we couldn't help but marvel at how it was run. Everything seemed to run like clockwork. If my wife and I hadn't both been communications experts, we probably would have been unaware of the mechanics.

The food was good, though, and we decided to return the following night to take a closer look at this operation. I interviewed the waiter to find out how much of the act was orchestrated, and how much was spontaneous. He was surprisingly frank.

The waiter admitted that the restaurant was based upon a very elaborate set of principles and practices. Each waiter was accountable for the yield from a particular table over the course of an evening. If the average yield from a table was only twenty dollars, when it should have been thirty, the waiter would see this disparity the next night on a board hung in the kitchen area. Waiters were taught certain phrases to encourage consumption of expensive items, and a "perfect" customer would be persuaded to have cocktails before the meal, wine during it, and be escorted to the disco, for more drinks, afterward.

This description probably seems off-putting, in some ways. There is no question that the restaurant could be a turn off for some people, but most customers, on a given night, seem to appreciate the attention and novelty delivery by the staff.

The example of this restaurant should demonstrate that restaurants are not so much in the food business as they are in the sales business. They owe their existence and prosperity to encouraging and cleverly guiding customer purchases at a given time.

NONPROFIT SELLING

The American Red Cross serves a vital function in society, by educating the public about health matters, assisting troubled populations, and by storing supplies of blood for emergency usage.

The Red Cross is also squarely in the business of selling, although it would perhaps not consider this to be a mission. To attract blood donors, the Red Cross often calls people on the phone to make direct appeals. They are selling in the sense that they have to initiate the contact and persuade prospects of the benefits involved in giving something of themselves.

They also have a difficult task before them. Apart from the fact that a donor might feel some satisfaction from giving of him or herself, there is little to encourage donations, and much to stand in the way. To the extent Red Cross personnel see their purpose as selling, they will be successful in creating the results they want.

With the diminished impact of the post-war baby boom upon colleges, these institutions have found that to survive they have to increase their base of support. Where enrollments once constituted the major source of revenue for schools, alumni gifts and sports, as well as community education programs now pick up the slack. Colleges are now exploring various ways of marketing educational services, although the concept of doing this was alien to them a very short time ago.

Political campaigns have always relied upon volunteers to get out the vote, raise funds, and build community support groups. This sort of civic persuasion is nothing more than selling in a nontraditional context.

EVERY EMPLOYEE A SALESPERSON

The best run companies in the world deliver one message to their employees: "You are all responsible for how the community reacts to us. Talk us up. Tell people you are proud to work for us. Even if you aren't in the sales department, tell people how much they'll enjoy owning our products."

I have had the opportunity to train customer service and sales departments in major corporations. One thing I have found in some of the largest firms is a narrowness of perspective on the part of people who work in given divisions. People in customer service are reluctant to see themselves as salespeople. They insist that selling is something that they have nothing to do with. They often find they grow depressed as the day wears on, because they hear complaint after complaint, about failed products and broken promises, and after being assaulted in this way, customer service people tend to believe some of the bad things they hear. As a result, they are afraid to sell an angry customer, although this would probably be the best thing for all concerned.

My company recently introduced a program to a large electronics firm that taught customer service reps to sell angry customers. The first step in the process was to take care of the reason for the complaint call, *and then to resell the customer on the desirability of the initial purchase*.

One of the lines they were taught to use is, "The Waverley is a wonderful device, though, isn't it?" Almost without exception, customers will resell themselves on the wisdom they had in buying the product to begin with. Their voices become animated and friendly, and they grow receptive to hearing about associated products to buy.

A marvelous thing happens to the customer service rep who engages the customer in reselling himself. The rep finds that his or her own attitude is boosted by the pleasant comments elicited from the customer. Instead of having the call end on a sour note, the call comes to a positive close.

"WHAT ELSE?": ORDER-TAKING VERSUS ORDER-MAKING

When you walk into a delicatessen in a major city, you are in for a sales treat. Walk up to the take-out counter, and order anything. You are likely to see the counterperson put your item into a sack, turn around, and flatly ask, "What else?"

If you are like me, you'll probably look around quickly for another item and say, "Uh, potato salad, please." This won't deter the counterperson, though, who will ask, "How much, one pound, two pounds . . . ?" Hearing these grand weights, you'll sheepishly say, "No, uh, a half-pound will be fine."

The counterperson says "What else?" You say, "That'll be it," and the counterperson, with a tone of real surprise will ask, "That's it?"

Whenever I go into a deli, this exchange seems to take place. I walk in with the idea that I'm going to buy one item, and I walk out with several items I never intended to buy, but which seemed totally appropriate by the time I left the place. Moreover, I always feel that somehow I should have purchased more.

Why do I do this? Because of those two lovely little words, "What else?" The counterperson is much more than an order taker—he or she is an order *maker*. If he or she can persuade us to buy just 15% more than we intended, on the average, the profits of the place will jump tremendously.

Many of us are in the position where we can influence a purchasing decision and encourage people to sweeten the deal by ordering more or various products and services. This is often a good place to start in cultivating our selling skills in a supportive situation where people are already buying from us.

GETTING SUPPORT FOR YOUR PROJECTS

Selling occurs whenever people want to get things done through others. If you have projects you need to fulfill, the primary means you will employ to engineer cooperation will be by selling those around you who can help out.

If people are convinced there is some benefit in doing something, they are likely to do it, and if they aren't, it won't get done. This is what salespeople do, by and large. They identify benefits and overcome resistance to new ideas and new ways of doing things.

I recall working on a consulting project where my company was introducing a rather dramatic change into an organization. The person who hired me was a staffer with about ten years of background with the company, and very savvy in getting things done. At the beginning of the project, we had a series of briefings and meetings with various levels of management to introduce the new program. With each group of people, my contact made a point of indicating the benefits of the program to them, in language that they could understand. He was literally selling the concept of the program, with group after group, in order to achieve the consensus needed for making the project a success. He understood that the only way permanent change would be produced would be through a process in which people got involved and became committed to mutual objectives.

SELL YOUR WAY TO THE TOP

Selling is a marvelous profession. It is a means of earning unlimited money, if this is your wish, and a person can lead a very comfortable life through reasonable effort. As I have heard it said, "A salesperson will never have to worry about finding a job," because there is always room in an organization for somebody who can generate business.

Selling is particularly attractive to people these days because it is a fairly concrete and straightforward job. One doesn't necessarily have to be a technical expert to do well in selling. In fact, *people skills* are of greater value in getting the job done.

Entrepreneurs are really people who are sales and marketing experts. They search for new ideas and products that have high profit potential, and then they sell these concepts to venture capitalists and the public at large. The rugged independence of entrepreneurs is due to their ability to sell their ideas in the marketplace.

If you examine the background of many of the people who make it to the top in their own businesses, the fundamental skill that all of them cultivated was selling. Without sales, their empires would have remained sand castles.

YOU HAVE HIDDEN TALENTS

I have trained thousands of people over the years to be salespeople. Many of these folks didn't think they had what it took to make it in this field. They believed the false idea that not everybody can be a salesperson. As long as people are willing to try, they can definitely learn the skills required for being successful in sales.

If you like meeting people, you already have a good start. A large part of selling is putting yourself before as many buyers as possible, and making these people feel at ease with you. Even more important is training yourself to understand the basics of a sales presentation, including the language that motivates people to buy.

When you use *winning language*, which is geared to encouraging people to buy, you will find that selling can be great fun. It is amazing to see how certain fundamentals come to your aid in the great majority of selling situations.

Ultimately, your greatest asset will be yourself and your own personality. You will find that you are able to sell people who are like you, right away, because they will identify with you and trust you. After awhile, you will be able to reach out to others who are very different because you are able to sense the communication style necessary for persuading them to buy.

The process of communicating with different kinds of people is a growth-experience that broadens us as individuals. By working with all kinds of people, we are likely to find that our personal worlds grow, while the distance we put between ourselves and others becomes less pronounced.

THE SELLING SOCIETY

American society is quite unique. Our economy is based upon countless sales transactions every day. If people decided to take a vacation from selling, our world would grind to a halt.

I remember speaking to a friend of mine about the prolonged economic recession America was experiencing. Being a sales veteran himself, he had an interesting perspective about America's diminished commercial vitality, and the emergence of Asia as the new productivity capitol of the world.

"Gary," he said, "America has forgotten how to sell." This seemed like exaggeration, at first, but he went on to explain this remark. "Major companies have forgotten what it takes to close deals," he pointed out. "They think they can 'buy sales' with fancy promotions and a lot of glamorous advertising, but the thing that really moves goods and services is one person effectively persuading another."

He went on to say that people didn't want to go into selling as a career because it didn't have the status associated with other callings. Few business cards bear the word, *salesperson*. Most business cards use other terms to disguise what the person does, when in fact, he or she really is a salesperson. *Investment counselors* and *customer consultants* abound, but there are few people who own up to being salespeople, however much these people are needed to perform this important function.

Salespeople are not only the instruments through which businesses distribute their products and services, they are the conduits through which consumers express their reactions to what is produced. When salespeople encounter tremendous resistance or acceptance, this is a clear signal to their sponsors to do certain things and avoid others.

Salespeople are also educators. As products become more complex, salespeople are being called upon to become technical experts, to understand their wares. They need to be communications experts in order to translate this knowledge to consumers.

Salespeople are also the first to ride a wave of change. They are the people who introduce new methods and techniques to consumers and professionals. Pharmaceutical salespeople are excellent examples of persons who introduce new medicines and devices to doctors. The doctors might otherwise not have the time to discover these life-sustaining means by themselves.

WE ARE ALL SALESPEOPLE

Some of us may be more effective in sales than others, but we are all salespeople, whether we think so or not. When I go into one of my favorite restaurants and I want to get a little more sour cream on top of my meal, I have to sell the waiter on putting in a good word with the chef so he'll be generous with his ladle. When you want a raise in pay or a promotion or you are searching for another job, you are most assuredly selling yourself and your track record. If you are persuasive, you win, and if not, you lose.

The key to selling is to be aware of the many techniques available to us for structuring an effective appeal and handling the resistance that inevitably comes our way when we try to accomplish new things.

The remainder of this book is geared to helping you to refine your selling skills in both traditional and nontraditional situations so you can make the most of the opportunities that come your way.

chapter two

How to put your best
self forward

Jerry Lewis is one of the finest comedians America has ever produced. His characters really hit home. One in particular stands out for me. It's the fellow who tries to act very suave and ends up botching everything. I think of this hapless character when the image of a typical salesperson comes to mind. Many salespeople try so hard to be sophisticated and controlled that they miss the mark entirely in delivering satisfaction to customers and scoring sales.

If there is one thing all salespeople need in order to be successful, it is *credibility*. Prospects need to find the salesperson addressing them knowledgable, organized, poised, confident, and compelling. In short, a good salesperson seems to know what he or she is talking about and is able to communicate that knowledge in an effective way.

BUILDING CREDIBILITY RIGHT AWAY

Credibility isn't necessarily something that takes a great deal of time to establish. In fact, if we are subtle, we can make selling easy for ourselves through a few simple steps at the beginning of a customer contact.

Who Do Customers Believe?

Customers like one thing very much in salespeople. If a salesperson *seems to be like the buyer*, half the battle may be won without further effort.

Joe Girard claims to be the world's greatest automobile salesman. Besides possessing very refined selling instincts, Girard makes a point of communicating one idea to his customers: that he is just like they are. He'll run after a prospect who is about to leave the car lot without buying, and say to the person something to the effect, "Look, I'm just like you are, and when you're ready to buy a car, it would make sense to buy from somebody you can relate to, right?"

This may seem like an overly simplistic appeal, but it works. There are more subtle ways of telling a customer that we are of a *like kind*, which we will explore. It's important to note that communication scientists have determined that in many cases 9/10ths of credibility is being liked by the buyer. One of the best ways to be liked is to be like the buyer.

Look-A-Likes

Have you ever walked into a hardware store and seen salespeople wearing three-piece suits? Probably not. It wouldn't be appropriate because the salespeople wouldn't be able to relate to their customers, who are probably wearing a little bit of the same paint they are looking to buy.

By the same token, we want to dress reasonably in the eyes of our customers. A designer suit may seem like a good idea when we buy it from the store, but it could also be considered too dressy for certain clients.

When I was in the automobile leasing business a number of years ago, I had a client who insisted on getting white station wagons. Nothing else would do, as I was to painfully discover, after trying to put him into a beige car.

This fellow had a specific idea about what his clients would accept when he drove up to their doorsteps. You see, his product line consisted of sprinkler systems for farms, and naturally, his prospects and clients were farmers. Farmers, according to this fellow, were very, very conservative, and the last thing they wanted to believe was that my client was making too much money on them. White seemed to look less expensive than other colors, and so it was chosen above the rest.

It's ironic that this same client of mine happened to own a Cadillac

Eldorado and a Rolls Royce, which he drove on his off-hours. When he drove up to farms, though, all his clients saw were white Chevy's.

How Should You Look?

Much material has been written about the subject of dressing for success. Some of the tips to be found in articles and books in this area are valuable. For example, it is not in good taste to wear a polka-dot tie with a checked shirt.

I think we get into trouble when we try to come up with one standard of dress that is desirable for all people, whether they work in offices, institutions, or in the field. The world will not be a better place if we all look like clones, with our gray, dark blue, or black suits, white shirts, and silk neckties. We need to develop a style for ourselves that suits our personality as well as the expectations of our clientele.

Here are some of my basic tips on clothing that have helped me to get along well across the country when dealing with all kinds of organizations and personalities.

Hair Styles

Have fun with your hair. If you deal with young people, they'll love your sense of spirit if you are a male and you allow your hair to grow slightly longer than the standard business length. If you are dealing with older types, they may feel you are a little restless, but they *will* notice you, and the first step in selling anything is in getting the prospect's attention.

Females should not hide beautiful hair in buns, pony-tails, or in any manner that diminishes attractiveness. As Zero Mostel said in "The Producers," when you've got it, flaunt it!

Make-up and Cosmetic Surgery

We should do anything that will help us to feel good and which will make other people comfortable with us.

Make-up should be applied sparingly. People who wear make-up should not look like the characters in the old "Flash Gordon" movies.

If you are dealing with a youth industry, such as the music business, you may be considering cosmetic surgery to reduce wrinkles and tighten the skin. If done well, it can make one feel and look better, which in turn can improve sales performance.

Clothes

Preppy clothes have endured in America for 60 years, or so, which isn't a bad run, when you think about it. Men really can't go too far astray when shopping at Brooks Brothers or similar type traditional clothing stores. These sorts of shops still have old-fashioned tailors and salespeople who know what they are doing. Just walk in and they'll dress you. Vested suits will probably be in style for some time to come, so you can't go wrong by selecting this style. Females look very good in preppy clothes, as they confer a youthful look to all.

I also suggest, in keeping with these guidelines, that clothes should be slightly larger in fit than you may think. This allows for comfort and an unintended bulge here and there.

Wear comfortable shoes. Wingtips aren't necessary, unless you like them. Choose a style that goes well with your style of dress.

Pick a Uniform If You Like

I started my own company by conducting seminars through universities and corporations. I fell into wearing a navy blue blazer with gray slacks and loafers. This was such a successful outfit for me that I wore it to all of my programs for several months. It saved me a lot of time in the morning, and I found it was universally accepted.

If you find a style you like, that becomes you, buy three or four of it at a time. Put two away for a future year, and get another in a different color. You'll be happy you did, especially if you are able to take advantage of a special sale.

Accessories

A leather briefcase is a solid investment. Cross pens are also well regarded, but be sure to purchase the 14-carat model. The cheaper model has a conspicuous tip and the silver model simply doesn't rate at all.

Jewelry

Make it real, whatever you do. Fake gems and fool's gold won't make you feel like a winner. Buy the real thing, or nothing at all. The most impressive pieces are custom-made, like initial rings, keychains, and necklaces. Don't waste your money on faddish items like gold razor blades for neckwear.

Of course, you won't want to wear too much jewelry. One ring per hand, one necklace per neck, and one bracelet per person is sufficient.

Casual Dress

It's difficult to be casually dressed without diminishing our personal and professional image. For this reason, it is advisable to invest in relatively expensive casual-wear, including cashmere sweaters, distinctive outerwear, and leather accessories. Men and women should always consider carrying a good sweater *and* natty sportjacket wherever they go. This will enable you to make even jeans look snappier.

Cars

Like most Americans, I love cars. Not enough to trade them in every couple of years, but enough to invest a good sum in those I think will have lasting value.

My clients think I should drive a Rolls Royce; at least this is what they say a big-time consultant needs for the old image. Who knows, maybe I'll give in one day, and get one. Those same clients will then claim I charge too much!

The cars we drive do tend to tell a story about us. I hired a person once to work with my company in the area of image development, and my impression of the person dropped several notches when I saw a beat-up contraption parked outside the door that the worker was actually proud to drive.

It is generally wise to drive a car that is slightly better than what you are used to driving, as this will make you feel good. Stretch a little to make the payments, and make the sales necessary to pick up the tab. If you drive a Chevy, you may want to move up to a Buick or an Olds, and if you have a VW you may want to try a BMW. If your clients will never see your car, ride a bicycle, instead!

A GENERAL WORD ON HUMILITY

I'll never forget the words of wisdom imparted to me by one of the best sales trainers in America. He said, "Nice and humble does it every time." He meant people can feel slighted or feel inferior by "high-hat" sales treatment. No matter what clothing or accessories we choose, we don't want to make our clients feel badly about themselves, because they won't reward us for bringing them down.

At the same time, I feel it is important to point out that we can become overly humble, and try in vain to change our personalities to suit each passing prospect. This can get out of hand, too. You'll find that there is a middle ground in appealing to customers that will enable you to be you.

BUILDING TRUST

There are few products and services in this world that literally, sell themselves. In most cases, salespeople are needed to point out the benefits of items where they aren't already obvious to the customer. Few customers will reward a salesperson with a purchase if they distrust him or her.

Trust is a bridge that we build to others that enables them to take reasonable risks in buying from us. How can we cause somebody to trust us if we have never before done business with that person?

One way is to make the customer *feel* like we have had a long-lasting relationship, even if it began only moments earlier. How do we get to know people? They tell us something about themselves, and we do the same for them. This exchanging of information gives both parties the feeling that they have background together, while it gives them the chance to see where they share common attitudes.

If I am trying to get to know a prospect, and I may tell the person that I have high hopes for the California Angels this year, and she says she has the same spirit, we are on our way. I may then choose to tell her that I am an Angels booster because I used to play in their organization on a rookie team a number of years ago. If she is a real baseball fan, this will open a number of conversational avenues between us. She will get the sense that the fellow who was a total stranger a moment before, isn't really all that bad.

Telling somebody about ourselves is the surest, fastest path to building trust. When we are open with another person, we don't seem like we are trying to put one over on him or her, or taking advantage of him or her in any way. Salespeople who do that sort of thing seldom bother to reveal themselves or their background to prospects.

In the long run, of course, trust is reinforced by fulfilling our claims and promises. If we fail to stand by our products, we won't earn the trust or respect that is so important in forging long-term, profitable relationships.

COMPETENCE

No matter how much we self-disclose, or seem to be similar to a prospect, if we don't appear competent to handle the person's needs, we'll fail. Credibility and competence are almost synonomous terms.

I assume that you already know your business in respect to all of its particulars. The problem occurs when customers don't know—you know! What we need to do is put customers at ease as soon as possible in the sales process so they don't ruin the interaction.

I do a lot of consulting for major corporations and large institutions. I have found that the people I coordinate my programs with are often unusually paranoid about the success that will come from my efforts. The fact that they have numbers of testimonials before them praising the work of my company doesn't put them at ease, either. They want first-hand proof for themselves that I am going to do a bang-up job for *their* firm.

I understand all of this, intellectually. But when it comes to getting down to implementing a new marketing program at their company, their concern can telegraph a message to their peers that the project may turn out to be a bust, and this puts a pall over the whole enterprise. When they finally discover that we did a great job, despite the negative send-off, they are impressed, and everything is fine. We can't undo the fears that were originally aroused, though.

This is why it is not only important to *be* competent, but to *appear* competent as well. The best time for this to take place is at the beginning of the transaction. If we fail to establish our expertise right away, we can get so wrapped up in noticing the prospect's lack of confidence in us that we become *de-skilled* and we blow the transaction because we have been thrown off of our game.

Important Tip: If you feel that your prospect is really nervous about you, tell yourself it is his or her problem, and not yours. By getting agitated, you won't help things along, and you'll only tend to make things worse.

What are prospects looking for when they express nervousness or anxiety about working with us? Reassurance. We need to tell them, through one device or other, that they are in good hands, and to relax.

Following are some pointers for projecting an image of competence.

1. *Control the sales interview from the beginning.* Sales are often lost

because the seller failed to set an agenda at the beginning of the interaction and stick to it.

The fellow I buy my suits from is a good example of controlling an exchange right away. When I walk into his store, Walt greets me and says it is nice to see me because he just received a shipment of suits that represent a terrific value, and he has already selected some great shirts and ties to match. "Let's look at the suits, first," he says, "and then we'll look into the other items, okay?"

Showing me to the rack with a sweeping arm-gesture, Walt suddenly asks, "42-Long, right?"

There is no question that he is in total control from beginning to end, and I don't mind because I get some great clothes, and his sales style is very efficient for both of us.

Let's examine Walt's procedure for a moment. After he greeted me, he created a sense of urgency by telling me that my timing was good because he "just received" a shipment. A well-tempered sense of urgency sells because it says, "Act now, or forever regret what you'll miss."

Walt then forecasted how the transaction was going to take place. First, I was going to look at suits, then shirts and ties. Notice that I no longer had the power to wander aimlessly through the store, because the order of my meanderings had been orchestrated by the salesperson.

This concept of telling a sales prospect where we are heading is a very good idea in most selling situations because it creates clarity and a sense of direction and purpose.

2. People believe in numbers, so have good statistics available for immediate reference. Statistics are powerful tools in selling, despite what people say about the fact that they can easily distort them and lie with them. It is a fact that people love numbers. Look at the great number of retail store windows that boast of "25–50% Off" the regular prices. This always seems to build traffic because people want to find bargains and because they have a fundamental belief in the truth represented by numbers.

If your product lasts longer, is cheaper, or in any other imaginable way represents a good value that can be put into numbers, by all means present it to customers this way.

When I persuade companies to purchase marketing programs from Goodman Communications I may tell them that we will double their productivity, judging from the impact we have had on other firms in the past. All they have to do is have a reliable measure of their current productivity level and take another measurement after we have implemented our program.

3. *Project a sense of self-confidence right away.* Do you know what self-confident salespeople do more than just about anything else? They *smile*. That's right, they have a big grin pasted on their faces because they are successful and are happy to be selling. This is a very important point.

When I am considering the purchase of some product or service, the last thing I want to do is get it from somebody who looks like a loser, with a sour expression on his or her face. When I buy, I am reaffirming for myself that I can afford the purchase in the first place because I trust in my ability to replace the dollars I spend.

If I am dealing with a sourpuss I am going to feel insecure about my decision to buy. Negativity is contagious, just as is enthusiasm. If a salesperson unwittingly projects a lack of confidence, I will consciously or unconsciously pick up on this and withdraw from the sales situation empty-handed.

Smiling is wonderful, anyway. I like going into stores where somebody, usually another patron, shoots me a negative look. I try to light up in return. A funny thing happens at that point. The frowner either smiles back, or averts his or her gaze. Both ways, I win!

I recognize that you may not feel like smiling at a given time. Too bad! Do it anyway. It's really a lot of fun.

4. *Get your body into the act.* As a professional speaker, I appreciate the importance of gestures in making a presentation interesting for an audience. We truly are our own best visual aids and sales aids if we will only choose to exploit our physical powers.

I participate in countless conferences that invite speakers to expound on various topics. One of the greatest copouts that a speaker can resort to, in my opinion, is relying on an overhead projector to do his or her work.

Overheads are very dull, I find, and when we lower the lights to make them visible, we put audiences and sales prospects into trances.

Physical actions and gestures indicate confidence, sincerity, and competence. When your body is involved, you will find that you become calm very quickly, which enhances your sense of command over the situation.

Los Angeles has a weatherman on a local TV station who is a real phenomenon, Dr. George Fischbeck. "Dr. George," as he is known, is sometimes satirized for using too many sweeping gestures to dramatize the weather. Nonetheless, he makes the dullest day seem like a meteorological miracle by animating his verbal descriptions with grand bursts of movement. He literally *looks like the weather* as he discusses it, and this gives the viewer the feeling that what he is saying is important and worth listening to.

5. *Tell yourself you are ten-feet tall.* Usually, it's the other way around. We tell ourselves that our prospects are the real giants, and we feel like weaklings by comparison.

I was honored to be a member of an elite training unit that had the responsibility of processing some 18,000 senior level U.S. Navy staffers through a management training program a number of years ago. Among my co-trainers were several highly skilled females who were concerned about dealing with a very powerful, male-dominated, training population.

My female counterparts were taught how to carry themselves in such a fashion as to make themselves seem taller, generally more massive, and more powerful. They were first told to think of themselves as being more physically commanding, and to move their bodies accordingly. All of a sudden, formerly "petite" people were moving more slowly, with a much greater sense of power than I had seen before. What were the results of this training? The female trainers were ranked by attendees as highly as male trainers.

THE P.E.P. FORMAT

To help you signal the prospect about your direction in a sales encounter, I suggest you consider using the P.E.P. formula for organizing your ideas on the spot. This will not only enable you to seem organized right away, but it will help you to respond to objections and challenges effectively.

Following is an example of this organizational format at work.

1. Point: The P.E.P. format has three simple parts.
2. Evidence:
   a. You start with a main point.
   b. You then support it with evidence.
   c. Then you restate your main point.
3. Point: As you can see, the P.E.P. format has three simple parts.

Imagine you are trying to sell someone an insurance policy, and to demonstrate various features and benefits of the plan you used the P.E.P. format to tell the prospect where you are headed.

1. Point: There are three options I am going to explain to you Mrs. Smith.
2. Evidence:
   a. Plan "A" is a term-insurance policy.
   b. Plan "B" is a whole-life policy; and
   c. Plan "C" is a new mutual fund-investment policy.
3. Point: These are the three plans I will be discussing before selecting the one that is best for your needs.

How organized! This sort of prelude would certainly tell me that the salesperson knows what he or she is doing, and I can relax and listen to an informative and helpful discussion. Is there any question that the salesperson has complete mastery of the agenda and the information at hand?

Imagine using the P.E.P. format to get you over the hurdle of an unexpected question. What if the prospect asked, "Why should I buy my insurance policy from your company, instead of Bozo Life?" Here's a pretty good response.

1. Point: While Bozo Life is a fine firm, our customers are happy with us for a number of reasons.
2. Evidence:
   a. We have very reasonable and affordable premiums;
   b. We have very generous renewal terms; and
   c. We deliver the best service in the industry.
3. Point: This is why our customers choose us over Bozo Life and others.

THE POWER OF ASSUMPTIVENESS

One of the cleverest television commercials to come along in some time has the theme, "Sooner or later, you'll own Generals." They're speaking of tires, of course, and the text is accompanied by a very pleasant musical melody. What makes this commercial notable?

The ad is important because it is *assumptive*. It *assumes* that the viewer will indeed one day own Generals. It doesn't ask, speculate, or otherwise beat around the bush. It *tells* the viewer what is going to be.

The assumptive nature of this ad could be a turn-off for listeners if it weren't done so lightly, and if it weren't accompanied by such pleasant music. Its power resides in the fact that *it makes a purchasing decision for the prospect*. The commercial implies that the listener will inevitably buy, and the message he or she hears is simply a reminder of that fact.

In studying social movements that have taken place throughout history, I have found that this "argument to inevitability," as I refer to it, is the most significant persuasive appeal that can be adopted by people who want to create change. What this argument tells the listener is that the outcome is assured, and it is only now a matter of determining how to let it take place in the most peaceful and pleasant manner. When the powerful hear this message, they tend to ask themselves, why bother putting up resistance if we are swimming against an inevitable tide? In this way, change is accelerated.

Good salespeople are also assumptive. I know a fellow who is a self-made millionaire from having successfully sold pharmaceutical devices to physicians. He says,

> What I do is open my display case, look directly at the doctor, and say, 'You should be able to use about four dozen of these, and two dozen of these, and another five or six of these, right?'

My friend is aided by the fact that he is about six feet eight, and two hundred sixty pounds, so when he makes his recommendations, he is virtually "looking down" on the doctor.

Before you begin a sales presentation it is smart to indoctrinate yourself a little bit by telling yourself, "I'm going to get this sale, I'm going to get this sale, I'm going to get this sale. . . ." This auto-suggestion can have a nearly hypnotic effect upon you and help you to feel assumptive. When we discuss closing techniques in Chapter Four, we will talk about the specific language that you should use to sound assumptive and powerful.

IT *IS* HOW YOU SAY IT THAT COUNTS

There is a degree of truth in the adage that "it isn't what you say, but *how* you say it that counts." For the most part, we are very unskilled in fully exploiting the influence available to us through our voices.

Most of us are trained to "keep a stiff upper lip," and to "put on a happy face," to project the right image of ourselves in meaningful encounters. We aren't nearly so well versed in making our voices do our bidding to come across to others in certain ways.

According to nonverbal communication researchers, as much as 80 percent of our expressiveness with other people comes through unintentionally. The fact that we are nervous in a selling situation may be inadvertantly revealed through a trace of nervousness seen in a clenched fist, or even in a quivering voice. We're usually unaware of how we give ourselves away, and this is especially the case when it comes to voice tones.

When we first meet someone, what do we do? We are usually so busy composing ourselves and trying to coordinate the handshaking ritual that we fail to hear the person's name, and generally get flustered.

We should make a point of sucking a lot of air into our lungs so we can give the person a hearty hello. This will do more to impress the person than anything else. When you combine the big greeting with a firm handshake and strong eye-contact, you will find that you are very well received.

Typically, a louder voice suggests to someone that you are extraverted and self-confident, which are useful characteristics for a salesperson. If you meekly say hello to a prospect, you'll probably find that you get a lukewarm reception in return.

Use your voice to amplify certain points and to minimize the importance of others. Typically, the weakest point in a sales talk comes when the salesperson mentions the price of the product and then asks for approval of the sale. This is the time when otherwise strong voices suddenly weaken, and prospects grow fearful. Instead of making this the weakest part of the talk, we should consciously try to make it the strongest by making our voices sound light and enthusiastic.

By the same reasoning, we should minimize what might be considered negative points in our talk by making our voices softer when we utter the weak statements. For example, if the customer has to pay a small deductible portion of an insurance claim, I will probably sandwich this negative fact between two pieces of good news, and make sure my voice takes the "sting" out of the bad news. I might say, "The ABC plan is ideal because it provides very inexpensive coverage, while limiting your exposure to only the $50 deductible. This gives you maximum protection at the most reasonable price."

If you were listening to this explanation, you would probably not think that $50 is very significant given the way it was described. This is precisely the effect we want to create by lowering our voices at critical times to downplay negatives, and by elevating our volume to amplify positives.

ARE YOU MAKING PROSPECTS READ YOUR LIPS?

Many salespeople have fallen on their faces by using sloppy speech that is only partially articulated. You know sloppy speech when you hear it because you have to strain to make out what the other person is saying, and often, although you are unaware of it, you probably resort to reading lips to some extent to figure out what is being said.

Effective salespeople are *understandable*. Their speech is clear and free from impediments. They use their lips, teeth, and tongue to make intelligible sounds, and when it seems that someone is having difficulty understanding them, they slow down to make themselves more easily understood.

One of the best ways to test the clarity of your voice is to read an article from the newspaper or a magazine into a tape recorder and play it back to yourself. Do you have to strain to understand what is being said? Ask someone else to listen and to give you a frank assessment of your vocal delivery. Then use the tape recorder as a method of steadily building your vocal dynamism.

WHEN IN TEXAS, DO AS THE TEXANS DO...

One of the enjoyable aspects about being in the sales business is that we have opportunities to communicate with people from all walks of life and from all areas of the country. Sometimes our interpersonal differences can get in the way of communication and selling if we aren't careful to respect these idiosyncracies and actually use them in our favor.

People in Texas don't sound like the people in New York, do they? When a New Yorker tries to sell a Texan, or vice versa, barriers can be elevated very quickly because each region seems to maintain a stereotyped image of people in the other region. To overcome local biases, *we need to adjust our voices in a manner that will put other people at ease*.

For example, if a New Yorker is trying to sell a Texan, he or she should try to make his or her voice sound like it is down on the range, rather than in the middle of the Avenue of the Americas. Certain words should be d-r-a-w-n o-u-t to appeal to the person from Texas. This approach will increase his sense of comfort with the person from the East.

Other vocal tips apply, as well. If we are from the East and we are speaking with folks in the Southern states, as a general rule it would make sense to make our voices sound a little more "round" and "soft" to conform to the gentle manner of people from that region.

The same rules apply to the Southerner who calls people in Chicago. They should be prepared to speed up and speak up, as well, and not be put off by what might seem to be a little callousness. It's all in the game, so to speak.

BUILDING YOUR PROFESSIONAL STATURE

An excellent way to put your best self forward is to not even be on the scene in person. Besides telemarketing, which we will cover in Chapter Six, there are other ways of transporting your influence without bringing yourself along for the ride.

One way to build your stature is to develop a newsletter that is sent to existing clients as well as to prospective clients. In the newsletter you can talk not only about the services and products that you provide, but you can also run articles of a general nature that will be helpful to the readership.

There is a fellow in Glendale, California who sends a newsletter and has great results. He is a realtor, and every few months we receive a copy of his newsletter that informs us about interest rates and realty trends. The letter isn't a work of genius, but it does put this person in a very favorable light. At least *he* thinks he is knowledgeable in his field, and he has the courage to put his thoughts in writing for all to see.

Another way to keep your name in front of others is to clip articles from newspapers that have some bearing upon the business your clients are in. I know a college professor who does some consulting on the side. He is a compulsive reader, so he puts his habit to work by noting any items of interest to clients or prospects. He then uses a rubber stamp to overlay the article with the words, "Courtesy of William A. Smith." His readers appreciate his interest, and he is fresh in their consciousness. When they think of consulting, they are likely to think of him.

You may want to consider writing articles in trade and professional magazines about selling your particular product line. When the article runs, you will find that prospects pursue you, which is a nice change of pace. You can also make reprints of the articles and send them out to prospects to enhance your image.

All of these techniques will make you appear to be a real professional, and will remove you from the ranks of being "just another salesman." When I was growing up, I had the pleasure to have two great Little League coaches. Each fellow took time out from his daily business to attend to a group of motley nine-to-twelve year olds. One coach worked in a local automobile agency, and the other sold insurance. I'm convinced that the good will each generated by giving time to us was more than repaid by parents who expressed their gratitude in buying new cars and purchasing insurance from these fellows.

Joining sales clubs can also be beneficial from the standpoint of increasing your education and your network of contacts. You will find that having a support group of like-minded professionals adds to your feelings of self-confidence. When you casually mention your association with these clubs to clients, you will find they come to regard you as being more credible.

POLITENESS PAYS OFF

Courtesy is very important in selling. This is especially the case when we are performing high-level executive and institutional selling.

One of the ways we can develop our politeness is to substitute genteel phrases for harsh ones. Here is a sampler of good phrases and bad phrases:

Bad Phrases
- "Wait a minute, and I'll show you what I mean."
- "There's no way Acme can undercut us on this one!"
- "Hold on, while I get her for you."

Good Phrases
- "In a moment, I'll be happy to show you what I mean."
- "On this particular item, it would be nearly impossible to do any better."
- "May I ask you to hold?"

The negative phrases sound like commands very often, while the positive ones are framed in a more gentle manner of speech. The bottom list will accomplish everything that the top one will, but without causing the other person to feel in any way abused.

If you want a good source on manners, I suggest you look at an etiquette book at the public library. While much of it will be devoted to rituals in which you may have little interest, I'm confident you'll find some answers to questions you have always had, but didn't know where to look to discover them.

There are four words that are generally underutilized that may be the most polite words in our language: *thank-you* and *I'm sorry*. We frequently forget to thank our best customers for their business, and our neglect makes these customers receptive to the sales messages of our competitors. Call your customers on the phone, every now and then, and simply tell them how much you appreciate their business, and ask if you can do anything for them. They'll love you for it.

Thank-you notes and letters are very effective, too. People are impressed that you have taken the time to express gratitude. Should you make an error that in any way causes a prospect or client "heartburn," apologize for it quickly, and set forth immediately to rectify the problem.

We live in an information age, as so many office automation products remind us in advertising. A sure-fire method of being polite and courteous is to keep your clients and prospects informed about developments that pertain to projects in which they have interest. They will appreciate the information and your attention, and again, you will stay fresh in their memories when they are thinking of ordering new products and services.

SINCERE COMPLIMENTS WORK WONDERS

Most of us are quite susceptible to flattery. We all want to feel good about ourselves, and we tend to reward those who elevate our opinions of ourselves.

I remember walking into a client's offices in the East not long ago. As I moved through the spacious quarters I noticed that the environment was very functionally divided, while it was pleasing to the eye. I paused, as my guide was walking me through the place, and I said, "Nice office." He said, "We like it. It's brand new, you know. You should have seen what the old one looked like!"

I could tell that he was pleased that I liked the space because it was important to everybody who worked there. Your clients and prospects may have heard compliments before, but they always feel good.

I know some salespeople who will actively search for something to compliment, even if their hearts aren't "in the message." This can boomerang if the client sees through it, so I would rather you make sure you really feel what you are saying before saying it.

OVERSTEPPING YOUR BOUNDS

Everybody has a "body bubble," or an "envelope" of space around them that is their comfort zone. They don't like strangers to enter their body bubbles unless they have been invited to do so.

We can inadvertantly cause prospects to think less of us by intruding into their *personal space*. For many people, personal space is any distance within approximately two feet of them.

You will know when you have violated somebody's comfort zone if you see that the other person starts backing up as you advance closer to him or her. At that point, it is wise to stop where you are, and actually consider withdrawing somewhat to lower his or her threat threshold.

There are other ways to violate someone's bubble besides walking into it. Some executives are very protective of their desks and become resentful when outsiders use any portion of their desks for their own purposes. This means that you shouldn't clutter somebody's desk with your briefcase unless you ask permission to use it, or it is offered to you spontaneously.

People will sometimes stake out their territories with various markers that have the effect of saying, "This space belongs to somebody else, so keep off!" Books, paperweights, and other dense objects are used for this purpose.

I have found some notable exceptions to the principle that an invasion of personal space causes negative attitudes to arise. When I was in the automotive leasing business, I had to show my clients appraisals of the damage that they did to their cars over the two or three years that they had driven them. Invariably, this discussion deteriorated into an argument, where the client claimed that the car was in "perfect condition, considering it had been driven for 40,000 miles," while I had the responsibility of pointing out that the little dings in the doors would cost a few hundred to repair, and the car would require a complete repainting, which would cost a small fortune.

It wasn't a very pleasant part of my job, no matter how you looked at it. I made an important discovery one day. I had always shown the appraisal form to my clients across my desk, and one day I decided to get closer to them by sitting down by them in a vacant chair on the other side of my desk.

A miracle happened! Clients were still upset by the appraisals, but they weren't nearly as belligerent in sharing their feelings. Their voices were softer, and their resistance was lowered. I found that I was able to collect a lot more money with less effort by simply changing my seat. What was going on?

One customer summed it up beautifully and unconsciously when he said, "Gary, I'm not happy with what I'm going to have to pay, but at least I know you're on my side." He couldn't have been more correct in his observation, because I was directly by his side, which gave him the feeling that I was *on* his side!

A number of years later I explored the literature of nonverbal communication and developed my own theory: If we take on the physical aspect of a certain relationship with somebody, we will put pressure upon their attitude to come into conformity with our physical behavior. In short, if we look like we are physically "close," we will tend to think we are mentally "close" too.

We can go too far with this, though. Beware of actually touching prospects. Many people aren't equipped to handle this much closeness, and they will sometimes find touching behavior out of line and personally offensive. If they touch you first, it's another matter though.

MAKING PROSPECTS "COMFY" WITH US

Much of selling may be seen as removing obstacles to buying and little else. Customers are usually nervous about making purchases, especially when they are getting into technical products or where they have never bought from us before. What we need to do is lower a customer's anxiety level, while increasing his or her comfort level.

A great way of doing this is by getting the customer involved in the sales process from the very beginning. Have you ever noticed what magicians do with people who are invited on stage to assist them? They distract them from their craft by asking them to do something. They give them a loose rope to hold, or they ask them to tap with a stick on a top-hat, or anything of the sort. The confederate stops being an audience member, and starts being a partner in the act. He or she will actually help the magician to create the illusion, and will leave the stage with a sense of satisfaction, even though he has contributed to his own mystification.

Successful salespeople get clients involved in self-persuasion. They ask questions that yield persuasive answers. For instance, if I am trying to sell a marketing program I may ask, "Would it be helpful to you if your salespeople could learn to close more effectively?" I like this one too: "If each of your salespeople simply closed one more sale per week, how much would that be worth to your company?" If the prospect is a reasonable person, he or she will see that it makes sense to do business with Goodman Communications. Remember this principle: If you tell a client something, he or she will attribute the idea to you and will resist it; and if you *ask* a client a well-designed question, *he or she will say what you want him or her to believe, and own it as his or her own idea*.

When we discuss the "Anatomy of a Sale," in Chapter Four, we'll explore the technique of asking questions more closely. It is a skill that can approach the status of an art, when executed properly.

This chapter has explored how you can put your best self forward. Our next chapter profiles the personalities and characteristics of successful salespeople.

chapter three

Profile of the successful salesperson

Think about the very best salespeople you have met. What were they like? How would you describe their personalities? What did they do to encourage you to buy from them? There is a profile of the successful salesperson that we can identify and describe. The greatest salespeople are known for behaving in certain ways and for being certain types of people.

Over the years I have asked thousands of seminar participants, many of whom were expert salespeople already, to sketch their portrait of the winning salesman or saleswoman. What emerges is truly a superperson, one who is very perceptive, motivated, and dynamic. This chapter stands as a challenge to those of us who really wish to do well in selling, as we will want to embody many of these traits.

WINNING QUALITIES

Everyone seems to have a basic personality. Some people have personalities that are outgoing and exuberant, while the personalities of others are more withdrawn and shy. Is there any particular personality structure that fares better in the selling arena?

The Alphabet of Success

Great salespeople have so many good qualities that the best way to describe them is alphabetically. And, of course, there is no better way to start than with "A."

A–ttitude

Zig Ziglar, one of America's finest motivators, has coined a number of memorable phrases, but one in particular is vital for salespeople. Zig says, "Your attitude determines your *altitude*."

Having a positive mental attitude is of monumental importance in selling. People need guidance, and they will follow a leader who is an "up" person much faster than a "down" person.

Whenever people make a purchase, they are reaffirming their own continuing capability of spending and making dollars in the future. If we aren't positive people, we call into question the customer's wisdom in deciding to buy from us, or perhaps from anybody, and everyone loses.

If you want to achieve more than an ordinary amount of success in life, set your sights on targets that are ambitious, and think positively and constructively in an effort to realize your objectives. All great things started out as mere dreams once. Tell yourself you can do anything, even if your dreams seem far-fetched. I remember my father gave me the greatest gift in the world when he told me that I was capable of doing anything, if I wanted to badly enough. Whatever success I achieve in life is traceable to these positive words.

Give yourself a pat on the back. Think of all of the challenges you have faced and surmounted. Some of these things may seem minor now, but when you confronted them they were very meaningful. Recall how you felt as you emerged from these minor battles victoriously. Now take that same feeling of power and project it into the future. Tell yourself, "If I could do it then, I can do it now!"

I remember this advice whenever I face a really hard-bitten seminar audience. When I sense that I am dealing with a tough bunch, I simply close my eyes and tell myself, "Gary, they're not going to be any tougher than groups you've mastered in the past, so relax, get in there, and have a good time. Also, be thankful that life is at least giving you a few challenges." This kind of pep talk does me a world of good. Try it for yourself and I'm sure it will help you, too.

48

B–enevolent

Top-notch salespeople are really givers. They give much more than they get. They look for opportunities to go the extra mile and deliver a high standard of service. This giving may mean that they take a temporary loss in the sense that they service an account that will not, at least in the short run, pay them back for the time they invested.

Frito-Lay is a company that is known for investing in its customers. Salespeople will brave blizzards to replenish a few bags of potato chips on a grocery shelf, although it costs more in time, gas, and labor than those few bags will ever return in revenue. As you can imagine, though, it is just this kind of big gesture on the part of Frito-Lay that endears the company to its customers and distributors.

Through these kinds of acts companies and salespeople build customer loyalty, which pays off handsomely over the long haul.

C–losers

Read the sales section of the classifieds in the newspaper and you will find a number of ads requiring salespeople to be *closers*. What is a closer?

Closing is simply asking for the sale. As you know, closing isn't as easy as it sounds, because most people are afraid to ask for commitment from a customer for fear that they'll be rejected. There are ways of closing that are very comfortable for both the salesperson and client, and we'll discuss these methods in Chapter 4.

Closing is an ability salespeople need to refine because most customers won't close themselves. Customers need to be encouraged by someone else. Your productivity will be directly geared to the efficiency with which you learn to close, and as with most things, the more you do it, the better you'll get.

D–isciplined and D–etermined

To be a good salesperson, you need to understand how the Law of Large Number works. The more you try, the more you'll get. It is just that simple. The hard part comes when you find that you have made presentations to ten prospects in a row, and every one turned you down. At this point, you need self-discipline and determination to keep you going in the face of adversity.

There is an old expression that says, "There is no failure in life, but low aim." This expression applies to salespeople who are very talented and who do pretty well, but fail to achieve the success they could if they worked harder. The really great salespeople are extremely disciplined. They "plan their work and work their plan," and virtually nothing keeps them from fulfilling their sales regimen.

Good salespeople seldom give up in their pursuit of a deal, unless they are convinced there is absolutely no potential in the situation. I recall managing a fellow, Barry, who was an excellent salesperson and who had real courage. He wasn't afraid to speak to anybody because, as he saw it, the worst thing they could do would be to say no. One day Barry called a prospect on the phone, and the guy got so angry that he said, "Don't you ever call me again!" It seemed like the prospect was blowing up over nothing. In any case, Barry went on with his business and forgot about the nasty conversation.

The next day Barry got on the phone to make some contacts and before he knew it, he was making a pitch to the same fellow who had yelled at him the day before. Instead of hanging up on the prospect, or gracefully terminating his presentation, Barry moved right through his talk until he reached the conclusion.

To his amazement, he got the sale! What is the moral to this story? Someone may say no to you on Monday and yes on Tuesday for reasons of which you may be totally unaware. The key is to remain disciplined and determined, and you may find that your prospects finally, or suddenly see the merit in your appeal.

You'll also find that it pays to periodically check back with companies that have said no to you in the past. Often, the person who declined has vacated the position, and in his or her place there is a more receptive person. I can't tell you how many times this has happened to me, and how rewarding it is to close a deal where a door had once been closed.

E–ntrepreneurial

The dictionary defines an entrepreneur as "someone who assumes the risks of a business or enterprise." Actually, an entrepreneur is much more than this. He or she is a person who senses opportunities in areas where most of us are unaware that moneymaking possibilities exist.

Good salespeople cultivate a knack for probing into organizations to find selling opportunities. They aren't satisfied leaving a company with a single order, unless they have planted the seeds of future orders before heading back to their offices.

One of the best ways of developing entrepreneurship is by building referral business from your current accounts. If you can simply generate an average of two or three leads from each of your existing accounts, you can probably double your business in no time. There is some truth in the statement that the best salesperson is a satisfied customer. Use the contacts you presently have to build your business.

F–rank and F–riendly

Many people have a negative image of salespeople. They believe that some salespeople will say or do anything to get a deal, even if it means lying to customers. While it is unfortunately true that there are unethical salespeople, as there are unethical people in all walks of life, the real professionals distinguish themselves by being frank and forthright, even if it means they will lose a small order in the process.

My first sales job out of high school was in a clothing store on the famous Sunset Strip in Hollywood. At that time, the hippie revolution was at its peak, and the local headquarters of the streetpeople was along the Sunset Strip.

Needless to say, all kinds of people came into the store, and we carried a varied line of jeans and "hip" items to appeal to the avant garde and the "chic" people who stopped in to look around.

Two fellows owned the store, and they were both in their late twenties or early thirties. They were too busy having fun to spend a lot of time in the store. This left me in charge, and I loved every minute of it.

I suppose I was an unusual salesperson. When people would emerge from the dressing rooms with oddball outfits that weren't flattering to them, and they asked my opinion, I gave them the unadorned truth. They were looking for reassurance, I guess, but I felt it was in everybody's interest to be candid. I'd say something to the effect of, "I don't know if that item really brings out your strengths. We do have something that you may like even better."

I would then hand them something that was more becoming, at least in my estimation. What was the result of this frankness? As you may have guessed, people appreciate the truth, and they usually walked out with purchases that equalled or exceeded what they were going to fork over for the original selection.

Just the other day I had the pleasure of a frank experience from the other side of the counter, as a customer. I called my insurance broker and asked him for a rate on my automobiles. He checked various rates and told me what the damages would be. I mentioned that I had received a quotation by mail from another firm that would apparently save me a few hundred dollars each year. I asked him if he had heard of the firm and if they were reputable. After a quick moment of reflection, he said, "They're okay, as far as I know, and I can't beat their rate with a stick. I'd take it if I were you." I thanked him for his honesty, and felt very good that I had recently increased my homeowner's insurance through his firm.

Successful salespeople also try to be friendly. When I deal with a salesperson who is hostile toward me or who actually seems unfriendly, I take my business elsewhere, or I "go without" if that is the other option.

How can you express friendliness? Smile, be open with people, and try to act spontaneously. They'll reward you with purchases because they'll like being around you.

G–oal Oriented

I have noticed something that I find very interesting. When I consult for various companies that pay their salespeople on some kind of quota system, most people perform within 10 percent of the target. This means that the great majority of those on the sales crew will either achieve at a level that is 10 percent below quota, or 10 percent above. If a company changes the quota, the same relationship seems to hold true. What's going on, here?

People set certain goals, or have them set for them, and they may or may not reach them, but they seldom exceed their targets by a significant amount. If they have low goals, they'll end up producing at a low level, and if they really have to exert effort and stretch to make their goals, they will probably produce more than they ever thought was possible.

When I first went on my own as a full-time consultant, after having taught college for five years and having been a part-time consultant, my first goal was to put food on the table and make "a lot" more money than I had made as a professor. As you may know, professors don't usually make a bundle of dough, so it wasn't too tough to exceed what had been my standard of living.

After being in business for awhile, I wanted to really earn better money and upgrade my lifestyle, so I set a goal to double my income by the following year. I announced this target to my wife, who had a gleam in her eye, but an unbelieving look on her face.

We made it! The next year my goal was high, but we made that goal, too. The following year I fell short of achieving my target. I hate to think what would have happened if I hadn't set my aim as high as I did, because that was the year of the "Great Recession of '82," and we still outearned our previous year, while investing much time in research and development. A lot of companies disappeared that year, and we were thrilled not to be one of them.

H–appy

Show me a successful salesperson, and more times than not I'll show you somebody who seems very happy.

And why shouldn't they be? They are probably taking life by the horns and getting nearly everything they ever wanted, including material gain and personal satisfaction as well as social recognition.

Show me an unsuccessful salesperson, and I'll show you somebody who isn't smiling and who probably isn't very happy at all. Whom would you rather buy from? Someone who seems successful and cheerful, or someone who is down-in-the-mouth and depressed?

I–ntelligent and I–nterested

I believe a good amount of native intelligence is helpful to a salesperson, because he or she needs to respond quickly to a number of challenges in presenting appeals to potential clients. Salespeople should be amateur psychologists, and have a good feeling for the attitudes, needs, and values of their clients. They should also be able to think on their feet and anticipate the objections that people will send their way. Naturally, they need to be able to communicate effectively to make their knowledge comprehensible to others who may know nothing about the products and services being touted.

Sellers should also develop wide-ranging interests and be able to make intelligent comments about numbers of matters, if necessary. I know a fellow who is extremely successful in his own public relations practice in Century City, California. From his thirtieth floor office, he looks down on Beverly Hills and Hollywood and recalls his rise to the top. "One of the things I make sure to do,'' he says, ''is read about fifty newspapers and magazines every week, to keep me alert to what's happening in the world. That way, I can bring a lot of new ideas to my clients.''

Some salespeople refuse to expand their command of their fields because they think they know it all by virtue of many years of experience and a certain amount of success they have generated for themselves. These salespeople are shortchanging themselves because the only way to develop new skills is to hear new ideas. If we prevent ourselves from experiencing novel concepts and methods, it's highly unlikely that we will ever change for the better.

We should cultivate the appearance of being interested in our clients' problems and challenges. This attitude will encourage trust and we'll learn how to help our clients fulfill their objectives through our wares.

J–ocular

The dictionary tells us that *jocular* means ''witty,'' and ''jolly.'' Effective salespeople should be interested in putting customers in the right frame of mind in order to make purchasing decisions. When customers are afraid, concerned, or overly serious about a matter, it is nearly impossible to sell them anything. We need to add a light touch to the proceedings, and if this involves making a little joke now and then, it can help our performance.

At the same time, it's not wise to act like the negative stereotype of the salesperson who is so busy offending us with raucous jokes that he or she doesn't pay attention to the more pertinent details of a transaction. Accordingly, it is dumb to tell ethnic jokes because they demean everyone, including the jokester.

Striking the right note through humor tells us that a salesperson is professional enough to not take him- or herself too seriously, while remaining sensitive to the dictates of good taste.

K–inetic

Kinetic people are active, enthusiastic, and energized. They seem to be a little bit in a hurry because they are accomplishing about three to ten times what the average person is doing.

When we speak with prospects, we should seem to embody a certain degree of urgency. I tell salespeople to respond to a client who claims that he or she is busy with the phrase, "So am I, and that's why I'll just be a minute." That's right! So are *you*, if you are the sales dynamo that you can be. Who has time to waste when there are so many people who need our products and services?

When we seem full of energy, we tend to electrify our prospects and we give off a glow of success that tells our prospects they are doing business with the right person. On the other side of the coin, if we seem like we have all day to talk, this can be interpreted to mean that we don't have too many people lined up on our dancecards, and business is sluggish.

Try to remember this maxim: *Scarcity sells*. Go to a sale at a car dealership and ask about a car that you see on the showroom floor. What will happen? Nine times out of ten, a salesperson will approach you and give you a pitch. You tell him you have to think it over and start to walk away, until you hear the words, "I hope it's here when you get back!"

"Aw, come on, nobody's going to buy it between tonight and tomorrow morning," you respond.

"That's what they all say," the salesman intones.

You know you are being given an appeal to urgency, but what do you do? If you're like me, you ask yourself, how will I feel if I lose this particular car? In other words, you'll probably get very serious about the whole idea of buying *that particular car* because there is only one available.

When we act kinetically, we are saying to a prospect, "Decide quickly, because my time is valuable."

L–istening

Professional selling and effective listening go hand in hand. To serve the needs of clients, we need to shape our products and services to their unique requirements. To do so requires that we first have a clear conception of our clients's situation.

Most people are terrible listeners. I was trying to change an airline reservation at the airport a few days ago and the ticket agent was a "selective listener." All she was interested in hearing were remarks that confirmed her prior ideas and attitudes. When I tried to point out that I required special attention, she didn't hear my comments at all. It was, as the old saying goes, "like talking to a wall."

Research in listening tells us some startling facts. When the average person hears another person talk, about 25 to 50 percent of what is being said isn't being processed consciously. This means it's going in one ear and out the other. Why is this so?

Scientists tell us that our attention spans are quite short—in some cases we become distracted about every four seconds. Furthermore, if we don't like what we're hearing, or if the speaker seems boring to us, we feel we have a legitimate excuse to drift off into never-never land.

Salespeople need to fight these impulses and strive to be excellent listeners. One thing we can do after hearing a client speak, is repeat what we think we understood. Often, the precise idea that the other person was trying to get across will have escaped us, and the client won't mind filling us in on what we missed, or even what he or she intended to say, but failed to mention.

By asking questions we will also get involved in what is being said and we'll tend to stay involved. We should avoid having emotional words throw us off the track. I remember speaking to one client about my experience with another company. I made repeated references to this other firm. At one point the fellow I was speaking to said to me: "I want to tell you something. Every time you mention that airline, I think of it only in one way. They flew me over to Vietnam, and they fed us the most boring thing, over and over again." The name of the airline reminded my client of an unpleasant memory, and I had no idea until he told me. As a listener, he had to fight the association that came to mind each time I used the name. He showed he was a good listener because he subtly told me to stop using the name so he could comprehend what I was telling him without interference.

I find note-taking a very positive device to capture what is being said for later clarification and analysis. By writing what we are hearing on a pad of paper, we are also likely to see ourselves primarily as listeners, and secondarily as speakers. Further, we will probably make our clients feel important because we are taking great care to take things down accurately.

M—otivated

Nothing ever gets accomplished without motivation of some kind. Many of us work because we are motivated by a need to feed, clothe, and shelter ourselves and our families, as well as to enjoy some degree of leisure and security. Once we get a job, we tend to move from day to day in a particular routine that is fueled by habit and routine, more than by a strong dose of inspiration.

Salespeople are a little different, though. They need to be extremely motivated on a daily basis to begin a routine that often requires tremendous energy and stamina to execute. To overcome the obstacles that are daily staples of selling, salespeople need to be "pumped-up" attitudinally. Perhaps this is why salespeople are such avid followers of the "positive thinkers" such as Norman Vincent Peale, Napolean Hill, Robert Schuller, and Zig Ziglar. These writers and speakers are famous for being able to encourage others to realize more of their potential by concentrating upon their unique gifts, and by using enthusiasm and a positive outlook.

I strongly urge you to become an *inspiration addict*, and read some of the books written by these people. They have collected inspirational stories that will make you feel good about yourself, and the challenges you have accepted in deciding to cultivate your selling skills.

I find there are several things that help to motivate me. I like to look into the thoughts of other people on various subjects, and take their comments on various topics into consideration. Because I don't have the leisure time that I once had for this purpose, I take a shortcut. I pick up a copy of *Forbes* magazine and turn to the last page. Collected there are quotations from great thinkers, many of whom are or were successful industrialists. In any particular issue, the magazine will cover a theme with its comments. As I am typing this page, I am looking at a quote from William James that says, "Nothing is so fatiguing as the eternal hanging on of an uncompleted task." This little gem is inspiring me to finish this book! Another good source for quotations is *Bartlett's Familiar Quotations*, which may be found in larger bookstores and in public libraries.

When it comes to motivation, salespeople are different in another significant way from average folks. They understand that they are responsible for their own motivation. They need not only to be "self-starters," but also self-sustainers when the going gets difficult.

N–atural

We have all heard of people who are "natural born salespeople." As mentioned in the beginning of this book, salespeople aren't really born, they are developed. But they do need to seem natural, to some extent, to be successful.

We associate people who seem natural as being honest, forthright, and spontaneous. We feel we can trust them because they are aboveboard and out in the open with us. At the same time, a salesperson needs to be so highly trained that his or her techniques of persuasion don't become obvious to the buyer. If the techniques are too visible, they tend to become ineffective. A salesperson is like a good actor who can make us forget he is the famous Richard Chamberlain and believe, instead, that he is the Count of Monte Cristo or Hamlet.

O–ptimistic

Whenever salespeople initiate contacts with prospects, they need to be telling themselves, "I'm going to sell this one," even if the odds seem to be against them. Prospects often unload a lot of negativity upon salespeople as a defense mechanism against making a mistake in buying the wrong thing. A salesperson needs to be able to accept the negativity from a prospect gracefully, without endorsing it him- or herself.

When prospects utter negatives, they are really looking for reassurance that they are making a good decision, and that they won't have regrets later. One sales trainer claims that the true function of a salesperson is to assist prospects in justifying and rationalizing their buying decisions. To do so effectively, salespeople need to seem optimistic.

If I ask my stockbroker about the merit of a recommendation that his firm is making and he reacts with the words, "Well, let's see what happens to this one," or "It may move upward," I'm not going to be terribly inspired. If, on the other hand, he says, "We have high hopes for this one," or "It's looking very strong to us," he hasn't done anything more than boost my spirits, but this may be enough to induce me to buy.

P–unctual

The great head coach of the Green Bay Packers, Vince Lombardi, made a sales training film that I saw when I was in the leasing business. He coined the words, "Lombardi Time," to stand for his idea of how salespeople should deal with punctuality. The former coach urged salespeople to arrive at appointments fifteen minutes ahead of time. What was the reason?

Lombardi believed that in doing so salespeople would be telling prospects that the appointment was important enough to them to make sure they arrived on time. It would also show potential clients that the service they can expect after the deal has been closed will be smooth and efficient, as well.

Lombardi urged salespeople to set their watches to "Lombardi Time," which meant advancing them a full fifteen minutes. This would enable the "late-runners" to at least come in under the wire and not be penalized by prospects.

Q–uestioning

The art of asking good questions should be cultivated by all who want to do well in selling. Salespeople need to induce prospects to "own" certain propositions about the product. For instance, the buyer needs to believe that the product is valuable and that it is going to produce benefits.

Typically, salespeople *tell* prospects that a product is going to be good for them. This isn't nearly as effective as when prospects *tell themselves* that this is so. How do prospects persuade themselves? By answering the questions that the seller has cleverly devised for them.

Tom Hopkins, a very knowledgeable sales trainer, calls certain questions that a salesperson strategically uses, *tie-downs*, because they tie down commitment.

I'm sure you'd like an example of a tie-down, wouldn't you? It would really be helpful, am I right?

The last two sentences you just read were tie-downs, weren't they? You can tell why, can't you? Because they first make a statement, and then they encourage you to agree with the statement, don't they? In fact, I've been doing this very same thing with nearly every sentence, haven't I?

The point of all this is that the prospect will start to agree with us after hearing a tie-down. When she or he agrees with our statement, a self-persuasion process begins. After a series of mini-agreements produced through tie-downs, the prospect is prepared to agree to the overall arrangement.

Tie-downs are closed-ended questions, where we were looking for yes or no answers. Though, sometimes we will want to probe the customer's needs through the use of open-ended questions. For instance, we might ask, "What are the basic skills you would like to reinforce in your sales training program?" This would be a good question to ask to discover the prospect's "hot buttons," or most urgent needs. All we then have to do is show how our plan, or product, meets those needs. Salespeople often make a mistake in *telling* a customer what the customer's needs are. This approach can be not only inaccurate, but also agitating to the client.

When asking questions, as discussed in a later chapter that deals with salesperson versus client-centered selling, we are using a format often referred to as *consultative selling*.

R–esourceful

One of my clients is an organization in the hotel supply business. This firm uses telephone marketing quite extensively and effectively.

The top salesman is a resourceful fellow who gets away with what might be considered sensitive strategies when trying to get past secretaries on the telephone to speak with the decision maker. If he believes he is going to get a rough time from the lion at the telephonic gate, he'll tell the receptionist he is calling from a magazine or newspaper. As many bosses are egotists, they'll rush to the phone, thinking that their name and picture are going to be on the doorstep by the time they get home that night. Instead, they hear the salesman announce his real name and purpose while he makes a point of apologizing for any "misunderstanding" the receptionist may have made about his identity.

I'm sure this backfires on him every now and then. But with his attitude he has nothing to lose if he shakes the prospect up a bit, considering that the prospect was avoiding him to begin with, and he couldn't have gotten a sale that way.

Cal Worthington, the Southern California oddity in the car business, has a philosophy about selling that motivates him to dress up like a cowboy and wrestle with live tigers, ride elephants, and claim that "I'll even eat a bug to sell you a new or used car." Cal says that "To sell somebody something, you have to first get his or her attention." Good salespeople use imagination in not only getting but also keeping the attention of the buyer throughout a presentation.

What are some good ways of riveting someone to our sales talk? Stirring stories, statistics, graphics, and hands-on materials and devices do well. You also may want to start out by reinforcing a common belief. For instance, you could say, "We all believe in productivity, but the question is how do we increase it without creating a host of personnel problems at the same time?" This sort of consensus statement can be quite effective in establishing your credibility as well because it tells the listener that he or she will be hearing something that is reasonable.

Another ploy is to use a startling statement to begin your talk. I might walk into a sales seminar and say, "In another few years what I'm doing here today will be completely obsolete. What powerful device could make a seminar like this passé? The same device that I am here to tell you about today—the telephone." I might then go on to speak about the link between the face-to-face meeting and teleconferencing and its relationship to face-to-face selling and telephone selling.

Powerful salespeople are constantly trying to make complex things seem comprehensible to their prospects. One great way of doing this is to alter people's perceptions about the scale on which they are doing things.

I was working with a client company in the airfreight business and I needed to motivate salespeople to do a better job. I believe that the staffers felt that their contributions couldn't turn around what was a pretty dismal financial situation for the company. I came in and said to them, "Look, don't think about all of the aircraft and people this firm has to support. Imagine we in this room are the only employees of this company, and we have only one airplane parked outside of this door. It's totally empty inside, and we have to fill it up with cargo, and fast. Our families and livelihoods depend on it. Now, if we were actually in that position, what would we do?" The answer I got was, "We'd fill it up!"

Another device that can be used quite effectively is the analogy, or comparison of situations that are otherwise not identical, but sufficiently similar as to allow for a similar interpretation.

A contact of mine in a client firm indicated that a group of employees in a distant locale needed sales training fast. She suggested that she get on a plane and try to do a rush job for them because "something was better than nothing." I disagreed, but the way I did it was by analogy. I asked, "If you felt ill and you knew you needed medication, would you take any pill that was within reach, out of convenience, or would you wait to use the specific medication that would help your problem?" She listened in total silence, smiled, and asked, "What do you suggest?" I suggested my firm do the training, and as it turned out, this person was quite persuasive in getting the project approved for us.

Another client of ours invited me to give a sales seminar at the company's home office. The official color of the company is green. I made a point of wearing a green wool coat and trousers as well as a green fabric tie for the presentation. The entire day went beautifully, and I have to feel that my matching of clothing to company-color helped to create at least a small sense of identification.

S–ensitive

At a customer relations meeting some months ago, I asked participants to describe the qualities in salespeople that they thought were least likeable. One general comment that captured most of the critiques was that salespeople were "insensitive." People were saying that the typical salesperson applies "too much pressure," and "doesn't know when to back off." What these statements told me was the least effective salespeople were almost oblivious to the feedback they were receiving from customers at any given point in the transaction.

When customers agree with our claims and support our appeal, they will tend to mirror our gestures and body orientations. This means if we talk with our hands in our pockets, customers will tend to imitate us, and when we remove our hands customers might unconsciously model our gestures and do likewise.

By the same token, if customers are hostile toward our point of view or are generally unreceptive to our claims, they will tend to avert their eyes so we don't establish eye contact. They might also lean back, thus creating more physical distance to manifest their psychological distance from us. They may speak in a measured tone, almost as if they are trying not to alert us to the intensity of their disagreement with us.

If salespeople are not sensitive to these cues, they can make the gulf between themselves and prospects appear to be that much wider and can make the consummation of a deal highly unlikely.

A salesperson should also cultivate a "sixth sense" for what is not being revealed by prospects. Whenever there seems to be an obstacle that exists that hasn't been explicitly mentioned to me, yet I sense its existence, I'll ask, "Is there anything else that I may want to take into account before we move forward?" Probing in this way can unveil problems that otherwise would have remained shrouded.

T–ime Managers

Time management is important for everyone who wants to be successful. When we take everything else away from ourselves that makes us differ, there is still one immutable force that makes us alike—time.

You have perhaps heard the idea that we shouldn't spend ten dollars worth of time on a twenty-five cent problem. Typically, though, this is what most of us do, and salespeople fall into time-wasting traps more than just about everybody else.

I am amazed by the number of large companies that support salespeople in the field whose function is to literally "beat the bushes" to find business. To better understand the marketing needs of one firm in an electronics-related field, I invested a few days on the road with some salespeople. We drove to various industrial parks, got out of the car, knocked on doors and asked people if we could get in to see the decision makers. As you might imagine, this was a terribly inconvenient method of doing business. Most of our stops were completely worthless as the people who made buying decisions were located in distant plants or weren't in their offices. For the people who were in, the responses to our uninvited calls ranged from chilly to frozen.

I recall that the salespeople who I ventured forth with would leave their cards and a brochure at all locations, even if the recipients indicate "zero interest" in the product. Salespeople would also insist upon getting the business card of each person with whom they spoke. I asked why they did this, and they said, "So I can send them a brochure and follow up with them."

I can't recall a less productive couple of days in my life! These salespeople were wasting time, gasoline, postage, printed matter, and their own energy by doing business in this way.

I ended up suggesting that most of the prospecting as well as selling be accomplished by phone, which is a subject explored in Chapter Six.

One of the major time traps salespeople fall into is pitching to the wrong people. These are people who aren't qualified to make a buying decision. Why do salespeople do this? In one sense, because it's easy. People who have no authority love to make themselves feel important by wasting the time of salespeople while they play the boss in a living fantasy. To overcome this problem, salespeople should first qualify the need for the product and the capability to afford it. They should further establish the responsibility for making a purchasing decision before getting bogged down in a fruitless presentation that can keep one from reaching truly deserving people.

As you'll see in later chapters, I urge salespeople to telescope the amount of time it takes them from the beginning of a sales ritual to its successful conclusion. I have found that a number of my clients make their way into a mature industry and blindly adopt the assumptions and methods that have been used without challenge for years.

I was working with a few Certified Life Underwriters in Indiana some years back who suffered from "hardening of the attitudes" when it came to analyzing their sales regimen. I asked them to narrate for me the typical sequence through which they solicited business. "Well," they said, "we first send out a crisp dollar bill and say to the prospect that this is an example of what we hope to make them through wise investments. We then call them to make sure they received it. Sometimes they ask for a few more samples! Next, we call them back and ask for an appointment to see them. Then we call to confirm the appointment before coming over. Then we call them after our visit to answer any questions they may have . . ."

I listened to this long list of behaviors, and I couldn't help but ask a purposely dumb question that consultants are known for: "When is the sale made?" They looked baffled. What did I mean? Was I being facetious? They couldn't tell me when the sales were made because they hadn't *planned a particular time to get the sales.*

I emphasize planning because it is crucial to our understanding of efficient selling. To be maximally effective, we have to explicitly plan for the moment when we will get approval for our proposals. If we leave it up to customers to decide if and when they would like to do business, we may be waiting a very long time for any action.

I suggested to my friends in Indiana that they should condense the amount of time and effort needed to go from initial contact to closed deal. For instance, there was no reason not to request an appointment on the same call when they were checking to see if their dollar bill had arrived. They should have also walked out of their face-to-face meeting with a signed contract, if possible.

U–nderstanding

Salespeople meet all kinds of people and need to find ways of establishing common ground with them so they can communicate effectively with one another. If a salesperson is constantly concerned with his or her world to the exclusion of "where the prospects are coming from," he or she will do a lousy job.

How can we develop our abilities to understand other people? One way is to ask ourselves what it would be like to be in their shoes. What would be most important to us, right at this minute? What would we be afraid of? To what would we be looking forward?

I was doing a sales training program for a real-estate company and afterward a fellow approached me. He asked if he could retain my company for the purpose of helping him to refine his strategies and improve his diction. He was from the Middle East, and his accent was noticeable but it wasn't keeping him from being the number one producer in his office.

I remember speaking with him about scheduling, and he said that he was going to have to return to his native country to sell some property before undertaking the training in California. I asked him why he needed to go back, and he ended up revealing to me a lot more than I expected.

He told me about his culture, the lack of food in the country, and how war had devastated a way of life that had once been very sophisticated. As he was talking, I came to feel that I was getting to know him on a level that would help me to shape my training to his needs. In essence, to help him to see the world "my way," through training, I first needed to understand the world "his way."

V–ictorious

A famous football coach coined the phrase: "Winning isn't the important thing—it's the *only* thing." I wouldn't be this extreme, but I do believe that truly successful salespeople have an irrepressable appetite for winning that spurs them on to greatness in the commercial arena.

My brother-in-law, himself a noted entrepreneur and self-made businessman, put it another way, "Anyone who loses and laughs, is an idiot!"

Good salespeople have their lighter moments, but they don't compromise their need to be victorious as soldiers of commerce.

Salespeople aren't beating clients in their sales victories as much as they are challenging their own records of achievement. A classicly motivated salesperson always wants to "beat yesterday" and set new records for him- or herself.

Some of the finest salespeople are ex-athletes who thrive on the competition found in the marketplace. Their early training serves them well when they encounter the numerous obstacles that need to be overcome in order to reach the top.

W–elcome

Truly great salespeople are nice to have around. They do little extra things for clients, like bring them news about what is taking place at other companies in the same industry. They may clip pertinent news articles and send them to clients "for their information." They may bring a client a bag of doughnuts, as a number of sales reps in the Midwest with a particular air cargo carrier are known to do. No matter what one does, it's important to try to go the extra mile to make a customer happy. If we do this, we'll always be welcomed, and our relationship will be secure.

X–enophilic

Effective salespeople love that which is foreign, new, and challenging, even if it is new language! Xenophiles are people who seek out new situations in which to test their skills and find new challenges. They aren't content to continually deal with known prospects, but instead strike out in pursuit of new business through new contacts.

Y–outhful

My dad used to say it, and by his behavior he lived it: "Selling keeps you young." Don't look to the Fountain of Youth or to magic potions if you want to feel youthful and vigorous. Selling can rejuvenate you as nothing else can.

The marvelous aspect about selling is that each encounter marks a new beginning. We never really know what fortunes are in front of us until we come upon them. This sense of mystery and intrigue makes the adrenaline flow and gives salespeople something to look forward to, each and every day.

Z–ealous

Stonewall Jackson said, "One courageous person makes a majority." This quote definitely applies to selling. The finest salespeople almost literally embody their products. They seem nearly inseparable from what they are selling. They aren't afraid of really getting excited about what they are doing, either.

When I'm selling, I'll often stop in the middle of describing a program we are designing for a prospect and will say to the potential buyer, "This is really exciting," or, "This is really going to be great." Almost without exception, my zeal for what I'm doing carries over to them, and they'll agree with me, right there, on the spot.

Many of us think that being zealous or nearly fanatically devoted to our products or services is somehow unsophisticated. In some cases, this could be correct, but in most situations, our belief in the product needs to seem unshakeable if we are to properly engineer consent.

These are some of the qualities that effective salespeople should possess. Selling gives all of us a challenge to continually try to elevate ourselves and never be satisfied to be exactly as we are at a given moment.

The next chapter shows you the actual mechanics of a selling transaction, from beginning to end.

chapter four

Anatomy of a sale

Given the profile of a successful salesperson discussed in the last chapter, you might be thinking that such an ideal person has never walked the earth. At least we haven't seen too many people who embody such lofty characteristics. Most salespeople, unfortunately, are poorly trained. They learn their craft either by the seat of the pants or by observing old hands who are, themselves, pretty poor models for imitation.

Ask a good salesperson how he or she approaches a sales prospect and you'll hear a definite answer. Good salespeople know what they are doing second by second, and few things are left to chance as the interaction unfolds.

If we examine selling in almost any field, through any modality, whether it is communication on a face-to-face basis, over the phone, or through the written word, there are essentials that cannot be denied. As with any good story, which has a beginning, a middle, and an end, a successful sales transaction follows a sequence involving five steps. We'll discuss the anatomy of a sale after we examine the types of prospects and what motivates them.

THE CUSTOMER MATRIX

Customers are often ranked by salespeople in terms of high-potential, moderate-potential, and low-potential in order to help sellers to manage time efficiently and assure that they aren't wasting their energy on the wrong people.

Ranking customers results mainly from a quick judgment made by the salesperson, and is based usually on a number of unreliable factors, including whether the salesperson *wants* to try to sell a particular person or organization.

I have developed a more systematic method for describing customers for the purpose of efficiently allocating time, which I call the Customer Matrix. It is a set of ten basic customer traits each broken into three subcategories, resulting in a total of thirty descriptive factors through which we may evaluate the potential of dealing with certain accounts.

The matrix is intended to be used as a device for determining not only with whom we should bother investing time, but also *how* we should conduct ourselves when we are dealing with different personalities. You will be able to score your prospects on various dimensions, and assign a grade that tells you how to deal with them efficiently.

THE FIRST DIMENSION: ENERGY

One of the most visible personality factors that any of us can evaluate is the energy level of another person. Do they speak and move quickly, or are they slower to react to things that you say and do?

We can judge people to have one of the following:

1. High energy
2. Moderate energy
3. Low energy

When trying to sell to these different types of people, we should try to match their energy level, which will make them feel comfortable. If we have high energy and the prospect has low energy, we may come across as overly aggressive and have our message rejected.

THE SECOND DIMENSION: INTELLIGENCE

Psychologists have argued for many years about what constitutes intelligence, and whether it can be properly measured. Nonetheless, I suspect that many of us can get a feeling for whether a prospect is really bright and with it, or whether we are dealing with a slower individual.

Do prospects follow your message closely and seem to be understanding you? Do they ask questions that show that they are relating what you are saying to what they already know? Are they ahead of you or are they somehow falling behind?

We can evaluate customers as having one of the following:

1. High intelligence
2. Moderate intelligence
3. Low intelligence

If we are selling to very intelligent people, we can presuppose an ability to understand new information quickly, so we don't have to spend a great deal of time on preliminaries. When dealing with people of moderate intelligence, we are wise to repeat ourselves periodically to allow them to grasp what we are trying to get across. When dealing with people who don't seem very intelligent, we should move slowly, and make a point to translate nearly everything into examples with which they can relate.

THE THIRD DIMENSION: OUTLOOK

People may be seen as being optimistic, realistic, or pessimistic, as general predispositions toward events, ideas, and projects. When dealing with optimists you can afford to give them what is called a *one-sided message* as your sales appeal. This message tells them only the positive or *pro* reasons for buying. You shouldn't bring up any negative arguments such as, "You may have heard that we had trouble with this model in the past, but I assure you that we've really worked the bugs out." This would be unnecessary when dealing with optimistic buyers.

When you present your appeal to realistic or pessimistic buyers, it is wiser to use a two-sided message that defeats the negative preconceptions that they may have harbored. If you don't, they are sure to bring them up as objections, and you may be at a weak moment in your talk when they do.

THE FOURTH DIMENSION: INNOVATIVENESS

Salespeople have as their number one purpose *the introduction of change* into the lives of people and the companies they work for. When trying to change the habits of others, we often encounter resistance from those who are reluctant to try new things. At the same time, there is a certain percentage of people willing to "take a flyer on something" and support a new product or service simply based upon assessing its strengths.

People may be categorized based upon the speed with which they embrace innovations. Rogers and Shoemaker, in an interesting scholarly book, *Communication of Innovations* (New York: Macmillan, 1971), identify several classes of people who exercise different adoption patterns relative to new ideas.

I have condensed their five-part classification system into three types of innovators.

1. Early adopters
2. Mainstreamers
3. Laggards

Early adopters are highly innovative. They are the type of people who are the first on the block to buy something new, whether it is a personal computer, a rotary or diesel automobile engine, or a time-share vacation purchase. In one sense, they could be called "trendy."

I deal with some companies that fit this description. They seem to hire more consultants than other firms, and they are among the first to implement suddenly popular management-training programs and the like. I find that their decision cycle is considerably shorter than that of other firms that aren't nearly as innovative. This means that I can press for early decisions after they have heard a moderate amount of information, and I will be likely to get results. An innovator or early adopter is also more highly likely to purchase by phone or mail because they aren't afraid of what appears as an "untested idea."

When dealing with early adopters, go for a "close" or agreement within the early stages of your involvement. I recall making a presentation to a security alarm company some years ago, and I didn't perceive them as early adopters and I lost the sale. The president and general manager were prepared to make a commitment during our first meeting, but I missed a cue that indicated I should have closed the deal at that time.

Mainstreamers are people who will wait until a product has some experience in the marketplace before making a commitment. You will find that these people constitute the majority of buyers in any general view of the American population, and when selling to them be sure to include in the appeal plentiful prior success stories from happy customers who have given testimonials.

Laggards are the last to take advantage of a sales opportunity because they are waiting until the price comes down, or because they are so insecure about change that they have to see overwhelming evidence that something is successful before they get on the bandwagon and agree to buy.

In a sales situation, laggards will be most likely to levy a lot of excuses and objections. Their favorite excuse is, "I want to think it over." Guarantees are effective with laggards because they ensure against the folly of a wrong decision.

There is a positive connection between the innovativeness and the general level of sophistication of a person. Early adopters are usually the best informed people, followed in order by mainstreamers and then laggards. This is one way to determine if you are dealing with a particular sort of person.

I have found that certain "objects" suggest whether a firm and some of its key employees are innovative. If I walk into an organization and observe that the people are using new, modern office equipment, which has been purchased more because of functions served rather than the name of the manufacturer, this tells me that I am dealing with a rather innovative environment. At the same time, if employees are saddled with prehistoric methods of getting their tasks done, I tend to think that the firm may be a lot more traditional and unreceptive to change.

I believe you will find that the cost of selling early adopters is substantially lower than that of selling either mainstreamers or laggards. Because the adoption cycle is accelerated, your time will be managed best by concentrating on this group of prospects, whenever possible.

Let's say you are interested in marketing a new product to companies. All the firms in America could use what you have to offer, but you want to concentrate on early adopters, if possible. Where would you look for them?

Your best bet would be to look into industries where change is most rapid. High-technology areas, such as computers and telecommunications, would be a good start. You might also look into the entertainment industry, and perhaps into the world of fashions. These types of organizations are trendsetters and are most likely to run with a new concept.

THE FIFTH DIMENSION: ENVIRONMENT

Environments are extensions of our personalities. A famous architect once said, "We shape our buildings, and then they shape us." Sometimes we can take a quick look at someone's home or office and get a feeling for the type of customer he or she is.

Three kinds of environments are apparent to us.

1. Elegant
2. Functional
3. Dysfunctional

By *elegant* environments, I mean something consistent with the dictionary's concept of an atmosphere of high quality, rather than one that is necessarily ornate. This means that furnishings are tasteful and are composed of materials that suggest quality; leather, wools, woods, and generally, "natural" or natural-looking substances.

An elegant environment may also be ergonomically designed, which is to say that it has been conceptualized with human beings in mind. This means that lighting and ventilation are sufficient and that chairs and desks have been chosen to make working physically less stressful. Some modern automobiles are ergonomically designed as they have literally wrapped the controls around the driver for added comfort, efficiency, and safety.

Functional environments are no frills affairs, where the basic word to describe them would be *dull*. Major corporate headquarters, with their seemingly endless corridors and linoleum floors are typical of a functional style. Things appear to be of uniform specifications in functional places. Offices, desks, and chairs are uniform, and individuals are usually not in control of personalizing their spaces with memorabilia or other artistic items.

Dysfunctional environments prevent people from being efficient. Desk surfaces are too small to organize the mountain of work to be done. There may be little sense in the location of certain items or departments. People are fitted to the building, instead of the other way around.

For an excellent description of dysfunctional architecture and its often fascinating impact upon attitudes and behavior, look into Robert Sommer's book, *Personal Space: The Behavioral Basis of Design* (Englewood Cliffs, N.J.: Prentice-Hall, 1967).

THE SIXTH DIMENSION: CLOTHING

Three styles of attire can be described:

1. Fashionable
2. Traditional
3. Convenient

How can we tell if someone is fashionably or traditionally dressed? Perhaps one of the best ways is to look at readily available guides published on a monthly or quarterly basis.

If you want to rate a male on this dimension, I suggest you look at three sources. Someone may be said to be *fashionably* dressed if his clothes seem consistent with styles that appear in the pages of *Playboy* or *Gentleman's Quarterly*. He may be termed *traditional* if his clothing choices would seem to fit into a Brooks Brothers catalog.

Convenient dressers are people who don't seem to have a consistent sense of color, pattern, or texture. If they look as if they just threw something together that morning, they probably did. When convenient dressers really "put on the dog," their clothes are likely to look either too small or large because they aren't used that often, and they have not been recently tailored. Moreover, dressers of convenience tend to shop in stores that promise economy, such as Sears, Wards, and the like.

For females, one may look to the pages of *Vogue* or *Glamour* for fashionable types, and to *Women's Wear Daily* for a sampling of traditional wear. As with males, females who dress out of convenience are somewhat insensitive to the impact of the blending of colors, patterns, and textures. Their clothes are also not very remarkable from an aesthetic point of view.

THE SEVENTH DIMENSION: DELIBERATION STYLE

Some people make decisions a lot faster than others, irrespective of the amount of information at their disposal. For those who make quick judgments, they are often very unlikely to worry about the wisdom of past decisions, because they are too busy, at present, making new ones. All salespeople appreciate prospects who can make up their minds, because they save us time and money and accelerate the purchasing cycle.

Buyers can be placed into three categories relative to their deliberation or decision making style.

1. Decisive
2. Moderately decisive
3. Indecisive

Decisive people wish to control the sales interview, and are not hesitant to steer it to a quick conclusion if they think they can do so effectively. They are often people who are looking for a little information to confirm or disconfirm a decision they have already made to purchase.

Moderately decisive people tend to balance the information they hear against counterproposals, and they are typically unlikely to assent to an agreement before chewing on it for awhile.

Indecisive people will often avoid making commitments of any kind, and are highly unlikely to return phone calls made with the intent of pinning them down on a particular matter. To complicate things, indecisive types feel guilty for procrastinating, so they tend to lead us on and make us think we have a deal when we don't.

To determine what kind of prospect I am dealing with, I will ask one of a few questions that will tell me what to expect. I'll ask, "What else do you need before we move forward?" If the person hedges and says, "Well, I'll have to think it over, and I'll be getting back to you," I may have a moderately decisive or indecisive person on my hands. Another effective bottom-line question is, "When would you prefer to get started, on the fourteenth, or will the twenty-fifth be better?" This is a choice close that narrows the possible courses of action to two. If the prospect is indecisive, he or she will try to avoid the issue altogether.

This kind of closing line may be uttered at the very beginning of a sales transaction to save us time and aggravation. I can ask a prospect this question going in to a presentation: "If what you hear and see is favorable, can you see any obstacle that would keep us from getting started right away?" Indecisive types will not give you a straight answer.

THE EIGHTH DIMENSION: PERSONAL STYLE

People may be classified according to the extent to which they seem to be personally stable and settled. They can be one of the following.

1. Secure
2. Moderately secure
3. Insecure

Typically, one's position in an organization is correlated to the degree to which a person acts and feels secure. People at the top are much more secure than their underlings. For this reason, dealing with principals and officers of companies is satisfying for a salesperson. Principals and officers are not usually afraid to act as they see fit, without the pangs of anxiety and remorse that inferiors experience when they are put in a purchasing capacity.

If you ever have a choice in terms of whom to sell to, choose the person with more authority. He or she will probably be less threatened by anything you propose, which could otherwise "rattle some cages" of people with less authority and perspective.

Insecure people are usually not worth dealing with, unless you have to. They bog us down in their own paranoia and tend to de-skill us by making us wonder if we have such a good product or service after all.

THE NINTH DIMENSION: AFFILIATIONAL STYLE

Akio Morita, the head of Sony Corporation, claimed in a recent interview that the reason America has fallen behind Japan in productivity is linked to the fact that we have become a society of justification instead of action.

Mr. Morita claims that Americans spend too much time in meetings trying to diffuse responsibility for their actions and as a result are less likely than in the past to get things accomplished.

You will find that some people in organizations express a great need to associate their actions with others in the firm. These kinds of people won't want to go out on a limb by themselves. Others are very likely to take full responsibility unto themselves, and still others are apt to seek the counsel or blessing of someone else before venturing forth.

People can be distinguished as one of the following.

1. Independent
2. Interdependent
3. Dependent

You'll find that *independent* decision makers are the most satisfying to deal with because they possess the power to get things rolling without obtaining the advice and consent of any number of others.

I believe it is useless to be satisfied after having given a single sales presentation to someone who is *interdependent* or *dependent*, because they won't be making the decision alone, and they aren't likely to be able to communicate the merits of your plan without immediate and sustained input from you. When dealing with these types of folks, make sure to find out who all of the people will be in making the ultimate go-or-no-go determination. Then set forth to communicate with them as early in the process as you can to line up their support for the ultimate approval of the project or purchase.

THE TENTH DIMENSION: PERCEPTUAL STYLE

People perceive reality in different ways. In fact, social scientists tell us that each person possesses his or her own reality, which consists of attitudes, beliefs, needs, values, and assorted information.

There is evidence to suggest that we actually tend to favor specific sensory modalities in understanding our worlds. For example, some people are very *visually* inclined, and for these people, "seeing *is* believing." Others are *touch* oriented, and they may be heard trying to "get in touch" with things, or trying to "get a handle" on some matter or other. Still others are *acoustically* oriented, and they put a great deal of stock in "what sounds right'' to them, while they keep their ''ears to the ground'' for signs of new information. People who are *taste* oriented are usually heard saying that certain concepts or sales appeals are ''hard to swallow,'' or are very ''palatable.'' *Smell* oriented people are constantly tracking the ''scent'' of something and often find themselves ''smelling something fishy'' here and there.

To be successful with prospects, we want to identify their preferred sensory modality. This is easily done by listening to the types of words they use most frequently in describing their experiences. Do they constantly refer to how they see things, feel about them, or about what they hear? If so, all you need to do to develop a little rapport with them is ''echo'' back to them the kinds of terms they are using.

People may be described as falling into one of three basic perceptual categories.

1. Integrated
2. Rational
3. Intuitive

Integrated personalities use both hemispheres of their brains in dealing with purchasing decisions. They see the surface qualities of a proposition in terms of its basic thrust, as well as its deeper structure of particulars. In other words, they not only have a gut reaction to a proposition, but they also tend to analyze its particulars with some degree of care.

Rational types see the proposal as something divisible into smaller units for analysis. They are the sort of people who will go over a proposal item by item and evaluate all of its components before giving you a decision.

Intuitive people act upon their feelings, primarily. If they get a good feeling about something, they'll go ahead with it, and if they don't get that feeling, they'll hold back. Intuitive people are quick to dismiss a message, based upon their mood or past experience with what they perceive as being a similar thing.

RANKING AND SCORING YOUR PROSPECTS

The Customer Matrix lends itself nicely to computation and interpretation. You will see the list of the following ten dimensions, and all you will need to do is score your prospects on these areas and come up with a total number of points for a raw score. After doing so, you'll then be able to interpret the raw score and determine how to best handle the accounts.

CUSTOMER MATRIX

Dimensions

1. Energy
   1. High   2. Moderate   3. Low
2. Intelligence
   1. High   2. Moderate   3. Low
3. Outlook
   1. Optimistic   2. Realistic   3. Pessimistic
4. Innovativeness
   1. Early Adopters   2. Mainstreamers   3. Laggards
5. Environment
   1. Elegant   2. Functional   3. Dysfunctional
6. Clothing
   1. Fashionable   2. Traditional   3. Convenient
7. Deliberation Style
   1. Decisive   2. Moderately Decisive   3. Indecisive
8. Personal Style
   1. Secure   2. Moderately Secure   3. Insecure
9. Affiliational Style
   1. Independent   2. Interdependent   3. Dependent
10. Perceptual Style
    1. Integrated   2. Rational   3. Intuitive

To develop profiles of your customers, simply circle the terms that you believe best describe them on each of the ten dimensions of the matrix. Each term is preceeded by a number. Add up all of the circled numbers, and this will give you a raw score.

INTERPRETING THE SCORES

10–15 points : Good Prospects
16–23 points : Average Prospects
24–30 points : Poor Prospects

As you can see, the lower the total number of points the better the prospect with which you will end up working. If you were to evaluate a prospect as a "10," you would probably be dealing with an ideal customer in my estimation. This person would be capable of making an independent decision based upon the available facts, and would be likely to give you instant feedback on your proposal.

On the other side of the coin, if you were dealing with someone who scored close to "30," I would abandon any efforts to deal with this kind of person right away, because it would be likely that you would be wasting your time with someone who was ill-equipped to make a solid deal within a reasonable period of time.

I recall working in the office supply business a number of years ago. As an independent contractor, I had the privilege of choosing whom I wished to sell, and how to go about it. I decided to deal with restaurants, and specifically with restaurant owners. My approach was to call the owners on the phone and encourage them to buy a significant number of items on the first call. My success was tremendous, but I recall that management wanted me to call other types of firms because they believed that the reorder potential was greater. I stuck to my guns, and continued to call my little cafes and prosper.

You see, the restaurant owners were very close to being "10's" on the Customer Matrix because they could make quick decisions without having to communicate with anyone else. Moreover, because they were in charge, they were able to quickly understand the merit of my proposal. They were, by and large, highly energetic, and they were innovative in the sense that they were willing to try something at least once. They came across as very stable and secure as well as perennially optimistic. In short, they had the best qualities of prospects, from the point of view of a salesperson.

If you already have been selling, think about your recent successes and failures. What kinds of clients were most profitable for you? Who gave you the toughest time? I suspect if you match your experiences with the Customer Matrix, you'll find there is a close connection between the results you have been getting and the kinds of prospects with which you have been dealing.

WHAT MOTIVATES PEOPLE TO BUY?

To understand the "Anatomy of A Sale." we need to delve into the area of customer motivation to understand what the "hot buttons" are that encourage people to buy. In using the right appeals, we will be likely to increase our success dramatically.

Needs

Everybody has certain needs that require fulfillment. Some needs are fundamental, such as the needs for food and shelter as well as medical care. Other needs are of a higher order, such as our need to socialize with others like ourselves, and our need to feel good about ourselves and our achievements.

If someone is concerned about where his or her next meal is coming from, it would be foolish to appeal to self-esteem needs. For instance, if we wanted to discourage poor people from stealing food from supermarkets, we would be wiser to show them that they could better serve their needs through constructive work than through stealing, which can deprive them of their liberty. To tell them that good people don't steal, wouldn't do much to deter them.

Similarly, I have found that in dealing with some organizations my contacts are less motivated by profits than they are by the power and ego gratification that come from introducing a successful new project into their industry. Telling them that a project is exciting, unique, and fulfilling will do me more good than bringing out a host of statistics about projected earnings.

Values

Values may be defined as goals that give our lives meaning and direction. There are twenty-one values that will motivate others to buy.

1. Prosperity

If people think that a product or service is going to increase their wealth, they'll go out of their way to invest in it. It helps salespeople to be as precise as possible in telling a prospect exactly how much gain to expect or savings that will be realized through the purchase.

2. Accomplishment

Some people work for more than money alone. School-teachers and college professors, for example, work for the sense of accomplishment they get from helping to develop the intellect and skills of others, while sharpening their own capabilities. There are people who will undertake very dangerous or taxing enterprises simply for the purpose of feeling that they have made a lasting contribution to their fellows.

Barney Clark was the first human recipient of an artificial heart. He underwent tremendous personal discomfort to pioneer a device that will undoubtedly save and prolong countless lives in the future. No one could claim that he did this for material gain.

3. Peace and Tranquility

Sometimes people simply want to be left alone, and they'll buy products that will make it possible for them to find peace and tranquility. Movie stars buy dark sunglasses or limousines with tinted glass to safeguard their privacy. As life becomes more complicated, people will be increasingly motivated by this value.

4. Beauty

Why do artists produce great works of art? For money? For fame? For immortality? Most artists are stirred to their craft because they are intoxicated by beauty. They want nature and various environments to conform to their conception of the beautiful.

If you think this is a far-fetched value, it really isn't. Robert Schuller is a minister who had a dream to build a "Crystal Cathedral" in Garden Grove, California. This cathedral would tower over the landscape and be a beacon to countless people. He thought his concept to build a gorgeous church was quite down to earth. When asked why he needed to build something so lavish and lovely, he responded: "Beauty is very practical because it is very motivating."

5. Equity

Most people want to do the right thing, whatever it happens to be in a given situation, as well as be the recipients of justice. This desire for fair play gives all salespeople a golden opportunity to open doors that might otherwise be closed to them.

I recall getting a sale when a fellow who had formerly been getting the business had "an inside track" with the people who decided where their dollars would be spent. Although I was warned that I probably didn't stand a chance in getting a deal, I still approached the organization and appealed to their sense of equal opportunity. As it turns out, I ended up getting the job after all.

6. Security

Some people will go to great lengths to feel secure. An earlier part of this chapter mentioned people in business who are *dependent* or *interdependent* and who are unlikely to make a purchasing decision on their own. One of the things we can do is make these people comfortable by anticipating their need to feel secure and by appealing to it. "Bill," I once said to a client, "this new marketing function is going to make you look like a hero, so I suggest you get behind it 100 percent." I was advocating the concept of *increased* security from taking a step forward, to counteract the conservative impulse security-minded buyers have when they are asked to do something out of the ordinary.

7. Freedom

I love the song, "Don't Fence Me In," because it seems so much in harmony with a basic American value, freedom. People want to feel that they have choices, and that in purchasing something, they will have increased options for doing things.

When retail salespeople show customers clothing, they often dramatize the strengths of a particular garment by showing how many different things can go with it. If we wish to be successful with clients we should make them feel that they are in control during and after a purchase, and that opportunities are opened to them through the process of buying from us.

8. Happiness

America is perhaps the only place in the world where the pursuit of happiness is the number one preoccupation of the majority of citizens. Ironically, though, if you ask people to define happiness they'll probably find it very difficult. They may say, "Having a million bucks," or "All the chocolate cream pie I can eat," or something flippant, but they'll have a more serious answer locked up somewhere inside of them.

Good salespeople try to get a sense of what will really make their customers happy. I'll ask this question directly, if I think it will help me to customize my product or service to the buyer. I'll ask: "If you could change any one thing about your sales staff, which would make your life easier and a little happier, what would it be?"

9. Love

Examine television commercials from an analytical point of view. What do a lot of cosmetics and clothing ads promise viewers? Love, sex, and attention. Love is such a potent motive that it helps nearly every product to sell.

I remember a very successful salesman in the auto leasing business a number of years ago. His office was next to mine, and whenever he'd reach a certain point in his sales talk with a prospect, he'd lean over his desk and soften his voice and say, "This model won't hurt your popularity any, either." He'd then smile, wink, and put the pen into the customer's hand for approval of the deal.

10. Pleasure

I think the best way to appeal to the motive for pleasure is to tell people that through your item they are going to have fun or a good time. People seem to take the governor off of their finances when they think that what they are going to be getting will be contributing to their pleasure.

I am always amazed at the difference that people, including myself, pay for First Class air fares versus some of the discount tickets that may be available at the same time. One reason people upgrade like this is because they have convinced themselves that they are going to have a better time in the first cabin.

11. Self-respect

People like to like themselves, and will go to great lengths to surround themselves with other people and with objects that make them feel good about themselves.

Why are dogs so popular? They make us feel good about ourselves because they are always thrilled to see us, and they show their affection through licking, wagging, and even smiling, according to some observers.

A sure way to kill a sale, by the same logic, is to prevent

people from feeling good about themselves. One of our clients is involved in a business dealing with customers who have called the company to complain about broken products. Our client handles their complaints effectively, and immediately turns around and sells them some accessories to go along with the broken product. How can this be done? By making them feel okay about their original decision to buy the product in the first place. If the customers continue to think that they were wrong in making the initial purchase, they'll be unlikely to want to hurt their self-respect more by repeating the unpleasant experience.

12. Recognition

I read a recent article by Robert Self, an executive placement specialist. He said that money doesn't motivate modern executives nearly as much as praise and recognition.

Smart salespeople will notice personal artifacts and objects that tell them something about the people to whom they are trying to sell. If an executive has a set of golf clubs standing in the corner of the office, the observant salesperson will make a comment about them because it is possible that the prospect will have a chance to boast about his or her skills on the links.

Clients also like to feel they are in good company. When I speak to certain clients, I'll make sure to mention the names of other "glamorous" accounts we have to make the person with whom I am speaking feel significant by association. A sincere compliment can also help you to motivate people by recognizing a strength they have or a contribution they have made.

13. Friendship

One of the benefits of doing business with people is that we can become friends with them, if we share mutual interests. By putting our business on a personal level, we can create a bond of loyalty that will help us stave off the assaults of the competition and realize opportunities that would be closed to us otherwise.

I have found that it helps to accelerate a relationship if we occasionally tell clients inside things that are off the record. This doesn't mean we compromise the integrity of our companies or ourselves, but we tell them things that they might not be able to hear from another source. If we preface our comment with the words, "As a friend . . ." we'll appeal to this value and create a tie between our clients and ourselves.

14. Understanding

I am an avid communicator in the sense that I live in a very verbal world. A number of people I interact with are also very wordy, and we don't hesitate to express our feelings and thoughts to each other. I have to remind myself that there are large numbers of people who don't really get much of a chance to express their ideas or feelings. They live in a more nonverbal world, by choice, habit, or necessity. As a salesperson, I have a chance to open them up, and give them an opportunity to be understood by someone else. This can fulfill a real need for the prospect, who will reward me with an order for the attention I give.

What is the key skill in giving another person understanding? *Listening*. Most people are grateful for a chance to be heard, even if we don't get around to agreeing with the point of view they express.

15. Convenience

If I were a physical scientist, I'd know a lot more about the laws of the universe. As it is, I only have a basic concept of how things work. One "law" that I'm very familiar with is that of "inertia." If we get something into motion, it takes a lot less energy to keep it moving at a certain speed than it did to get it moving in the first place.

This law certainly applies to human affairs, as well. As Chaim Potok, the novelist put it, "Beginnings are very difficult." People, in other words, are unlikely to break with the past unless there is a compelling reason to do so, or unless it is made *easy* for them. Salespeople function to create reasons. We provide good reasons for people to buy, and we need to make it easy for them to buy, as well. People are creatures of inertia and convenience, and if we don't get the ball rolling for them, they'll be unlikely to do it for themselves.

16. Consistency

People have a tremendous need to be right. Have you ever noticed how people defend the most outrageous things if they are being criticized? Why do they do this? To be right, and to avoid the stigma of being wrong.

One of these days I am going to create an audiocassette tape that has two words on it that are repeated by about one hundred different voices. What will the words be? That's right, they'll be, "You're right!" If I sold the tapes on the open market, they'd probably become best sellers.

The need to be right makes it foolish and self-destructive to argue or fight with clients. There is no way to win a fight, because the loser will still walk away trying to prove he or she is right.

This need presents itself to me whenever I introduce a new idea to industry. What is one of the first things I hear? "We've never done that before." The tone of voice with which this is said indicates that the speaker doesn't usually do anything that is inconsistent with the past. As a salesperson, it's my job to show buyers that the new practice may be different from what they are presently doing, but it is consistent with the spirit of their larger objectives.

17. Inclusion

I remember a song from the 1960s that went: "I'm in with the in-crowd—I go where the in-crowd goes . . ." This song summed up the need to be included of adolescents as well as their elders. We all want to feel included—that we are part of something larger than ourselves. Many of us dress a certain way, drive certain cars, and choose particular lifestyles because they fit in with our concept of what is chic, hip, or in at any particular time.

The need for inclusion is also related to our desire to be liked by other people. If we're liked by other people, they'll include us in their plans and want to be with us. Department stores that have unadvertised sales to which they alert their credit card customers, and nobody else, appeal to this need for inclusion. Simply adding a person's name to a mailing list can satisfy this desire, as well.

I know people who hate to go to parties, but who love to be invited, nonetheless. They could be said to have a slight value conflict between freedom and inclusion.

18. Excitement

Sometimes a desire for excitement can overcome a lot of competing wishes. I was dealing with a firm where we were introducing substantial change, and where senior staffers were quite concerned about the fallout from the venture. I reassured them, not so much by mitigating the possible down-side risks, but by referring to the excitement that the program was going to create.

People do crazy things because they are bored, or because they want to spice things up a bit. If you ever go house-hunting, you'd probably as amazed as I am by the kinds of things people do to their homes to relieve boredom. One place I looked at had a hot tub installed in the middle of a closed garage! Amidst the gardening tools and discards of the house was this bubbling spa. Somebody must have thought it would be exciting to have some fun next to his parked car, for some reason.

19. Getting What One Thinks One Deserves

The other night I had to catch a flight to a distant city, and I was working until the very last minute before leaving for the airport. I ordered a limousine to shuttle me the 40 miles to Los Angeles International, and it was respectfully parked outside my home when I was ready to depart.

I got into the back of the large Cadillac, and I put my stereo-headset on and listened to some classical music as we shoved off. All of a sudden, I felt a twinge of guilt. "Should I be spending the money I am on this limo, or should I have taken a cab, instead?" Without hesitation, I answered my own question. "I deserve it," I told myself, and I enjoyed the rest of the trip.

Sure, it was a luxury, but this is the way we rationalize our purchases of nonnecessaries. We pat ourselves on the back, and we spend. Salespeople who sell Rolls-Royces understand this process completely. They do everything they can to make customers feel that it is totally natural for them to be getting this very expensive car at this point in their careers.

20. Feeling Important

Perhaps the classiest barber shop in the world is Drucker's, in Beverly Hills, California. Its customers have included President Reagan, Frank Sinatra, Morey Amsterdam, and my father, Bernard Goodman.

I remember my first haircut at Drucker's. I was about to

graduate from grammar school, and my dad had set an appointment for me. I was a little afraid, because Drucker's was a very sophisticated place, and I thought I'd feel a little foolish there where I'd be surrounded by a bunch of elders.

My dad and I walked in the door, and Harry Drucker extended his hand, and in a booming voice exclaimed, "Hello, Young Goodman!" I was a celebrity! He expected me! A twelve-year old has never felt more important.

When people spend their money, they want more from the bargain than the bargain alone. They want to feel that they have a certain amount of power, that they're important, and appreciated. If we can make people feel important, they'll do business with us again and again.

21. Knowledge

Most people want to develop and grow, and the best way of accomplishing this is through learning. Our customers will often ask us questions that seem foolish to us, but they are really trying to learn something from the transaction.

Good salespeople tend to educate their clients without, at the same time, seeming like they are talking down to them. I have found that my clients appreciate receiving my monthly *Telephone Effectiveness Newsletter* because it fulfills some of their appetite for knowledge in a particular area.

NEGATIVE SELLING

These 21 values that we have identified can be aroused in a positive sense, by telling clients that they will receive satisfaction of these needs through the use of your products and services. At the same time, we can motivate customers by *negative selling*, which tells them that if they don't buy our goods they will be frustrated in having their goals realized.

Let's take the value of *understanding*, for instance. If this is important to a client who is shopping for consulting firms, and mine is being considered, I might say that we really understand their needs while the other companies couldn't possibly understand them as well, under the circumstances.

The motive of peace and tranquility can be stimulated by telling a customer that a failure to purchase your goods could result in a hassle at some point in the future.

In other words, if the satisfaction of a goal can be motivating, the prospect of frustrating that desire can be motivating, as well.

THE SELLING SEQUENCE

A sale should be an organized process of persuasion. Most sales will follow a five-part sequence.

Part One: The Opener

The opener is the attention step in which we gain the interest of the prospect. Usually, this step is poorly executed by salespeople, and this is nowhere in greater evidence than in retail selling.

Go into ten stores in your neighborhood shopping mall and start to browse through the racks. A salesperson will probably walk up to you and open the conversation with, "May I help you?" This is a dangerous beginning because it empowers the buyer to say "no." The people who might say "yes" are already pre-sold on buying something, so it doesn't really matter what we say to them. We probably won't discourage them. We are better off asking, "*How* may I help you?" This question asks for specific information from the shopper and assumes that we are going to contribute to an ultimate purchase, and all we have to determine in the meantime is *how* this is going to take place.

Another approach in a retail setting is to determine what styles the shopper seems to be settling upon, and direct the person's attention to some items of probable interest to them.

The thing to remember in retail openers is that they should be fast and nonthreatening. If we can open with a question that requires the shopper tell us what he or she has in mind to buy, this will be very helpful to our cause. Again, we should avoid a yes or no question. For instance, we don't want to ask, "Are you looking for a suit?" Instead, we should inquire, "What sort of suit were you looking for, something in polyester, or something in a natural fabric, like wool?"

People don't want to be sold, so they'll "flee" if we come on too strong in the opener. At the same time, they want to know that help will be available when they want it, so we should always try to remain visible and accessable to them.

There are several specific openers that can be used to break the ice with prospects.

1. Startling Statistic
   "Did you know that the average wear people get out of Goodman suits is eight years. That's pretty good, isn't it?"
2. Quotation
   "Artistotle once said, show me a well-made suit, and I'll show you a Goodman!"
3. Story
   "The last gentleman who bought a Goodman suit from us won the Irish Sweepstakes the next day. Think you'll be that lucky?"
4. Question
   "When you look for a suit, what's the most important thing for you?"
5. Historical Reference
   "*That* is the best suit that Goodman has ever made."
6. Special Sale or Bargain
   "Last week, that cost twice as much."
7. Third-Party Testimonial
   "My brother-in-law just bought a Goodman suit, and in two weeks he's gotten a promotion and he's been made Grand Hamster of the Woodchuck's Lodge.

   "He won't be seen in anything other than a Goodman."
8. New Product or Service
   "We just got that in. It's state of the art."
9. Demonstration
   "Try this vest on, and you'll see what I mean. It has b-o-z-o-s-t-r-e-t-c-h, a built-in comfort feature found only in a Goodman."
10. Inactive Account
    "Have you been on vacation or something? We haven't seen you in a long time."
11. Thank you
    "Ms. Smith, we just wanted to let you know how much we appreciate your business, and we also thought you'd be especially interested in this fashionable jacket from Rico Goodman."

After you have broken the ice with an opener, your work really begins. What you need to do is focus the interest of the prospect on what you have to sell. This may mean that you will help the customer to identify an existing need, or you may have to take the initiative and "create" the need for him or her.

Part Two: Identifying the Need

Perhaps the best way of identifying someone's need for your product is to ask the person some questions. If you can ask a sequence of "loaded" questions that cause the customer to persuade him- or herself, you will find that your job is made a lot easier.

As mentioned in a previous section of this book, there are two basic kinds of questions: open-probes and closed-probes. An open-probe is phrased in such a fashion as to require a full explanation from the person.

For instance, I might ask, "What kinds of tools will be helpful in training your people to sell more effectively?" This presupposes that such tools exist, that training is necessary, and that we will proceed if the prospect provides the requested information. It is then up to the buyer to fill in the spaces with information.

If I asked if you'd like your salespeople to sell more effectively, I would receive a yes or no reply that could serve my purpose if I wanted to find out if you were a serious buyer. If I received a "no" answer to this sort of probe, I would get the message that help isn't wanted.

Part Three: The Solution

The next step is to announce the solution to the problems or needs that have been identified. This announcement is developed in such a way as to demonstrate that it is a complete and comprehensive satisfaction of the customer's problems. "Given your needs, I believe a two-day training seminar will be just right for you."

Part Four: The Benefits

After announcing the solution, we need to point out the benefits that the customer will gain by adopting our product or service. Benefits are "deliverables," which is to say that they are statements pertaining to what customers will get or gain from our suggestions.

Let's say we are trying to sell someone limousine services. We will open our talk with a question: "How many times have you been stuck in traffic and wondered if there isn't a better way of getting places?" We will then proceed to identify the need: "The average driver in a metropolitan area spends fifteen hours every week commuting to and from work, and driving across town for business meetings. These treks are not only wasteful, from a productivity standpoint, but they drain our limited reserves of energy and keep us from doing our best."

Our solution follows immediately: "We have solved this problem through our convenient, inexpensive, and pleasant limousine service. We eliminate many of the obstacles that companies such as yours presently face."

Our benefits step tells the listener what he or she will gain from using the service. "When you use Goodman Limousine Service, you'll find that your executives no longer knock themselves out trying to finish paperwork after hours and on weekends, because they'll be able to get so much done as they travel. They'll also be able to entertain clients in the proper manner because the chauffeur will attend to the minor details of transportation that can be distracting at the worst times. You will liberate cash that has been spent on maintaining a large fleet of vehicles. You'll be able to do this inexpensively, while reaping the benefits of increased productivity across your entire staff. Moreover, there is nothing like the feeling one gets in a Goodman Limo."

Part Five: The Close

The close is the time when we get approval and commitment. There are three basic closes that I recommend.

1. The Choice Close

To get you rolling, all we do is set aside a date for the first service, and the schedule indicates a good time will be on Monday, the fourth, or will Tuesday, the fifth be better for you?

Note the phrasing here, because it is very important. The key to the choice close is that we are not asking whether they want to get the service started, but *when*. If they answer the question as it was posed to them, they will inevitably buy from us.

2. The Assumptive Close

> The best date to get you folks rolling will be on Tuesday, the fifth. Our chauffeur will arrive fifteen minutes early, as is our custom, and he will announce his presence to you at that point . . .

As you can tell, I didn't give them a chance to decline, did I? I simply *assumed* approval of the deal and went on to speak of inessential particulars of delivering the service. Although this is a very powerful way to close, you may not want to use it in all situations.

My friend occasionally shops at a snooty boutique that has sales every now and then. The last time they had one they called her and used an assumptive strategy that she ended up resenting. The salesperson said, "Now we'll look forward to seeing you, because everybody can certainly show up because we'll be open until seven that night." It just so happened that my friend accidentally splashed some chemical into her eyes and had to rush to the doctor, preventing her from going. She still associates this overly aggressive attempt at persuasion with the pain she suffered through the accident.

3. The Checkback Close

This is also a tie-down close such as the ones introduced earlier in the book. What we do is make an assumptive statement and follow it with a tie-down, right?

> The best date to start your new service will be on Tuesday, the fifth, okay?

The little "okay" on the end of the statement is pivotal in gaining assent and involving the customer in the decision. We are all conditioned to say okay when we hear okay, aren't we? We're also conditioned to agree with a question when it comes after the expression of a fact, isn't that right? The same logic makes the checkback close effective, doesn't it?

And An Extra Step For Assurance . . .

Sometimes it is advisable to add a step to the selling sequence for the purpose of assuring the sale we have made. What we do is simply repeat the particulars that have been agreed upon, and we should try to do this in a very matter-of-fact way.

Imagine that a buyer has just given us the go-ahead on a deal but we're unclear as to how solid the order is. What we should say is something similar to the following.

> Fine, Mary, now just so I'm clear, we'll be sending our limo by on Tuesday, the fifth, at 10:30 in the morning. Our chauffeur will be arriving about fifteen minutes early to assure that he'll be on time for you.
> "Do you have any questions? Well, I'd like to thank you, and we'll look forward to working together."

If Mary hadn't been completely sold on the service, she would have uttered her uncertainty during this "confirmation," and I would have had a chance to bolster the sale where needed. If I didn't allow her to express reservations, I may have received a cancellation without any opportunity of rectifying matters.

Trial Closes

Some sales presentations last so long that it is handy to close them at our earliest possible opportunity. This is where minor closes or trial closes come in.

Imagine you have just begun your sales talk and you have gotten through the opener and are about to move into the "needs" step. Before doing so, you decide to throw in a trial close to determine if your prospects have genuine interest in your goods. You ask:

> If I can show you how to make more money without any additional net investment on your part, this is something you'll want to pursue immediately, right?

If the prospect says, "No, we can't change anything about what we're doing right now," you'll have a good indication that the person isn't worth selling, or what you will have to address to induce the person to adopt your plan.

Some salespeople use a series of trial closes throughout the presentation in order to get the prospect in the habit of saying "yes." I recall looking over a health spa with the idea of joining a number of months ago, and the salesperson punctuated practically every benefit statement with a nod of the head and the statement, "And that's nice." Before I knew it, I started telling myself, "And that's nice," after each statement she made.

DON'T BE AFRAID TO QUALIFY YOUR PROSPECTS!

Many salespeople waste valuable time by failing to find out if a prospect has the authority to okay a deal and the financial means to execute it. They fail to get this vital information for two reasons. First, they are concerned that they will offend the buyer by questioning his or her abilities. Second, they are afraid to confirm what they suspected all along: that the really nice person they have been speaking to isn't in any position to talk with them seriously.

I like to use the question: "I understand you are the boss, here, is that right?" You can also try, "Besides yourself, who will we need to consult in order to get a project underway?"

As you can imagine, the best time to qualify the prospect is in the beginning of the transaction, before you have wasted your time.

THERE'S GOLD IN "THEM-THAR" INACTIVE ACCOUNTS

A tremendous source of sales leads may be found in your firm's inactive accounts files. You will be amazed at the goodwill that your organization has unknowingly created throughout the years that can be cashed into new profits and new business.

You'll also find one fact particularly pleasing. Those accounts with whom you had a little conflict or misunderstanding will, by and large, be amenable to hearing from you again, and in a number of cases, they'll place new orders with you right away.

Now, why would they want to do that? Memories are short, for one thing, and they are probably buying from another source beset with its own troubles, which are fresh on the mind of your buyer. Constant communication with clients, past and present, pays off handsomely.

MAKING YOUR CLIENTS YOUR GOODWILL AMBASSADORS

It's only partially true that "nothing sells like a satisfied customer." The fact of the matter is that most satisfied customers don't tell anybody about the commercial bliss they have found in our products and service. They remain silent, and our sales don't grow as they should. We need to encourage our happy customers to help us to make others happy, too. How do we do it?

The first thing to do is get testimonial letters from people who have been happy to work with us. The more the merrier, because some people will find certain letterwriters credible if they are from their industry or region, but they may refuse to believe someone else's kind words about us.

Here is another small roadblock: Most people are too shy to put their comments into words because they are self-conscious about their writing skills. No problem. Show them someone else's letter, or ask them a few direct questions about your product and service. For instance, you might ask:

1. "Mr. Jones, would you say this product was the best you ever used of its type?"
2. "Would you freely and enthusiastically recommend it to anyone who uses pots and pans?"
3. "If you had it to do over again, would you buy it?"
4. "If I asked you to sign your name to what you just very kindly said to me, would you do that for me?"

The next step is to ask for a piece of the person's stationery, sit down at the typewriter, and compose the following letter.

Dear Gary:

After having used your pots and pans I must say that they are the very best on the market. Not only this, but I would highly recommend them to anyone who eats food.

They have been worth every penny, and I am thankful that I took advantage of them when I did.

Thank you again, and good luck to you and Goodman Pots & Pans.

Sincerely,

William Jones, Sr.

As you already know from having read the Customer Profile, a good number of prospects will be impressed by testimonials and won't want to make a commitment to you without seeing some evidence that you have made others happy in the past. So, have plenty on hand!

You'll also want to "grow your business" by getting referrals from existing customers. Some insurance salespeople try to get the names of three other people from prospects *before* they do any selling, which is pretty challenging. I suggest you simply ask your clients for the names of two people who they think would be happy with your product or service. You'll probably find that your percentage of sales conversions will be very high because referral prospecting usually yields very good results.

ONE-STAGE VERSUS MULTISTAGE SELLING

It sometimes takes more than one encounter with a prospect to earn us the business. Some sales campaigns take a great deal of time to consummate. Advertising agencies, for instance might woo a client for years before finally getting the opportunity to be of service to them. For this reason, we need to match our selling cycle to the constraints of the industry within which we are working. A one-call close simply may not work if we are trying to sell large-capacity computers to businesses with complicated objectives and procedures.

At the same time, I suggest we always try to collapse the selling cycle whenever possible. A fellow in the computer business heard me speak a few months ago, where I was talking about the desirability of "going for the gusto" and closing at every opportunity, especially on the phone. The same day, this fellow decided to close a prospect on the phone, and to his astonishment, he did it. The prospect, who didn't expect to be making a commitment of this kind during a phone conversation said, "Why not?"

A definite part of learning to be successful in selling is in handling resistance, objections, and difficult buyers effectively. Chapter 5 examines these obstacles.

chapter five

Mastering objections and difficult customers

What is it, above all other things, that separates salespeople from nonsalespeople? Their stamina? No. Their backgrounds? No, again. The single most important difference between salespeople and nonsalespeople is that the professional marketer is trained in the art of handling resistance, objections, and difficult people.

Most nonsalespeople recoil the moment they hear someone utter some negativity, while trained salespeople learn to welcome objections. The pro knows that a sale really begins when some sort of difficulty is encountered. As a sales manager once said to me many years ago, "If you didn't have to handle tough customers, and if nobody gave you a rough time, we wouldn't need salespeople, would we?"

Professionals also tend to gear themselves for objections as everyday aspects of the job that require routine handling. A typical nonsalesperson behaves as if he or she never heard the negative remark before, and the prospect usually senses a lack of experience, and the sales is "blown."

Some salespeople actually learn to welcome objections, which may seem to the inexperienced like asking someone to hit us over the head with a baseball bat. Why would anyone invite resistance?

IT'S A PERCENTAGE GAME

An earlier chapter referred to the Law of Large Numbers, which says that if you try a sales strategy often enough, you are bound to experience at least some success. The person who welcomes objections is operating from a similar premise. Here's what it sounds like.

If it takes the answering of ten objections, on the average, to finally get us a sale, and a sale is worth one hundred dollars, what is each objection "worth" to us? Ten dollars, right? It's just that simple. The next time somebody says "no" to you, or gives you one of the basic objections which we will be referring to later, smile and tell yourself that they have just "paid" you a certain number of dollars, from a statistical standpoint. To cash in, all you need to do is persist, and from your efforts with several prospects, you'll find you are rewarded nicely for your exertion.

80 PERCENT VERSUS 20 PERCENT

If you examine the literature in selling and management, you'll find several *80–20 rules*. For example, it is said that on a typical sales team, 20 percent of the salespeople will produce 80 percent of the sales of the organization.

I have another 80–20 rule to offer you. If your firm is at all like the many companies I have consulted for over the years, you will probably find the following statistic holds true: 80 percent of your gross sales will be earned after at least one objection has been handled properly. That's right, 80 percent.

If you haven't been answering objections at all, which isn't unusual, I believe you are very possibly ignoring a large percentage of prospects who would buy from you if you took the initiative to manage their resistance.

WON'T I TURN PEOPLE OFF IF I ARGUE WITH THEM?

Yes, and this is why I will teach you to avoid "arguments" at all costs. Dale Carnegie put it well when he said that nobody wins an argument. If we attack someone's point of view, he or she will usually go to extraordinary lengths to defend him- or herself, even if clearly in the wrong.

But aren't we arguing with people if we are trying to deal with their objections? Not if we are well trained and we are doing it effectively.

WHY IS EVERYBODY ALWAYS PICKING ON ME?

In the 1950s there was a great tune called "Charlie Brown," and one of the characters in the song asked, "Why's everybody always picking on me?" It may seem like we are under seige when we first start selling because we're probably encountering more flak than we've ever seen before. Why are prospects so difficult? Here are a few reasons.

The Brat Inside All of Us

Some people get their jollies by making other people squirm a little because it reinforces their convoluted desire to be powerful. They can't "lord it over" anyone else, so they pick on a salesperson who is forced to be nice in order to get the sale.

When you come across this kind of person, you have a few options. First, you don't have to play along if you don't want to. If you think they are simply toying with you, you can say:

> I appreciate your interest in this product, but I sense a better time to discuss it with you will be in the future. Here is my card. Thank you.

If it seems to you that I just kissed this one good-bye, that may be true, and I can live with that if I must. We should remember one thing: We really can't win them all, and it's ridiculous to hold ourselves up to a perfectionistic standard that says we're less than human if we don't get along with each and every prospect. Remember the Law of Large Numbers: Talk to enough people and you'll meet more than your share of bozos.

Consumer Crusaders

We live in the Golden Era of the Consumer. Watch TV and nearly every station has an ombudsperson to whom irate customers can send their complaints in the pursuit of commercial justice.

People don't want to be suckers or "easy sales." They have been warned against making snap decisions to buy various things, so it's natural for them to tell us they're not interested, simply as a defense mechanism so they won't purchase each and every item that is offered to them.

Note here that they may *really be* interested, but they are playing a game in order to keep themselves from unleashing the pent-up consumer demand locked up inside of them. This game is really no different from the games that Americans play when we go south of the border, into Mexico. There, we play "bargain time," in which our goal is also not to be an easy mark, but we will dicker and ultimately say "yes" to a reasonable offer.

What I'm saying here is that you really shouldn't take someone seriously when they tell you they aren't interested in the very beginning of your sales talk. How could they be? They haven't heard enough yet in order to be interested, have they?

You're Being Tested

A number of customers think they're pretty sharp, and your sales appeal provides them with a forum in which to test their wits, and to "try" yours. I've found that these people are also salespeople, who are out to prove that they're really top bananas. They end up throwing the kitchen sink at you like a drill sergeant puts a recruit through the regimen. If you come up to snuff, they'll usually reward you with the order, and if you crumble, so will your hopes for earning a buck with them.

They Have a Problem with You

Some people don't like us, and there's not a whole lot we can do about it. They may have taken offense at the foreign car that we drove in their parking lot, because their brother-in-law is an unemployed steelworker, and your Toyota contributes to his misery.

They may not like the fact that you are sporting a beard, which they'd love to do, if they could. Or, they may instantly dislike you because you are "young" or "old" or who knows what.

If you think the reason you're not getting anywhere with a prospect boils down to the fact that they have heartburn with some part of you that you can't really change, by all means don't blame yourself, and don't try to be a chameleon just to please them.

Remember, it's their problem and not yours. Their simple-mindedness or closed-mindedness is a prison of their own creation, and they're probably serving a life sentence.

How can you tell if someone doesn't like you? Do they throw pies in your face? Seldom. What they do is give you scant information to go on with which to build an effective sales appeal. They may avoid looking you straight in the eye, because they fear you'll detect their displeasure. And they probably won't smile, although some of them will have cultivated the ability to smile and snicker at the same time.

The best tip I can provide is don't take it personally, even if you think it is personal. Remember the line from another classic song of yesteryear: "One monkey don't stop the show."

They Have a Problem with the Product or Offer

This area is where you'll get the bulk of resistance. People believe they have no use for what you have, that it's too costly, they have a substitute, or they don't have any time to discuss the matter with you.

We'll develop some specific answers to these objections later in this chapter.

They Have an Unrelated Problem That They Are Taking Out on You

This treatment happens more than I care to think. A fancy name psychologists give the phenomenon is "displaced aggression." Most of us recognize it as scapegoating. People are blaming you, unconsciously, for a problem they are having in some other area of their lives. What can you do about it? Two things.

First, you can be generous and tell yourself that your customer is responding to you out of all reasonable proportion, and there must be some reason for it, though you don't have to take it upon yourself to explore what it is.

The second approach is to clear the air and ask, "Is there another problem going on here, that I may not have taken into account?" I did this recently, and my buyer said, "Today just isn't my day, you'll have to forgive me."

THEY ARE NOT ALWAYS ANGRY, YOU KNOW

Nonsalespeople often mistake a number of responses for anger. Anger, by the way, is defined as "emotional excitement induced by intense displeasure." Keep this definition in mind as we discuss some common reactions that are mislabeled, "anger."

Fear

When people are afraid they express themselves in peculiar ways. A typical reaction to fear is aggression as a way of protecting ourselves from something that we find threatening. A prospect may seem angry with us and only be expressing concern about the proposed sale.

If someone is concerned, the best thing to do is offer reassurance. If we misinterpret fear for anger, we are likely to respond inappropriately ourselves. We're likely to increase a client's defensiveness instead of reduce it.

Disinterest

Some people are, by nature, more *intense* than we are. I have an in-law like this, and for years I misunderstood him because I thought he was the emotional equivalent of a bull in a china shop, when in fact he was a very sensitive, warm person. What threw me off? His *delivery*. He didn't talk as many other people did. He exclaimed things very passionately—even everyday things.

Disinterested people can come across in a similar way. They may *seem* more emphatic in their feelings than they really are.

Blunt Language

Folks who don't mince any words may not have that many in their active vocabularies. As a result, they may come across as being short with us when they don't intend to do so.

Don't take offense too quickly at what you think is a poor reception, and remember what my brother once said to me: "Given enough time, people will say almost anything."

Genuine Interest in the Offer

When we are feeling particularly defensive, as if we are under attack, we tend to take practically everything somebody says as hostile. This gets in the way of selling.

Imagine that you have just completed an unsuccessful presentation with prospect "A." This person really gave you a rough time, and you feel intimidated. Along comes prospect "B," who starts asking you a number of questions about your product or service. What are you likely to do? You're probably going to interpret the questions as challenges, and respond defensively. In doing so, you'll probably get your client out of the mood of buying from you.

DEFENSIVE MESSAGES

Our egos can get very involved in the process of selling, and they can lose a lot of business for us if we don't watch out.

One of the ways ego rears its "beautiful" head is in making us feel that we have to compete with clients. For instance, countless sales are lost because clients wish to feel *superior* to salespeople.

I once spent a day with a salesman for a very large vacuum cleaner company. This guy was a real mess. His tie looked like it had been chewed up by a pack of hamsters, his suit was about three sizes too large, and his shoes would be shunned by any self-respecting hobo. The minute I saw him I felt a little bit sorry for him.

We ventured to a house where the owner was in and the salesman proceeded to spill the contents of a vacuum cleaning bag on the pretty carpet before us. The prospect screamed, and said that she struggled to clean house and this bozo had ruined her rug. He asked one question of her: "It would take a pretty strong vacuum to clean this mess up, wouldn't it?" Through her amazement she said yes.

He plugged in his machine and quickly made the carpet as good as new. As he was doing this I couldn't help but notice that the prospect was checking out his clothes, and she wasn't impressed. Before I knew, it, though, he had a signed contract for the vacuum cleaner and we were off to another demonstration.

This fellow turned out to be the best salesperson on the staff. He certainly didn't dress for success, or maybe he did. I think people don't want their vacuum cleaning salespeople to look affluent, although they may want their lawyers to look that way.

Clients sometimes need that feeling of superiority. Unfortunately, many of us react very negatively when we think someone is talking down to us or patronizing us. As salespeople, we would probably be wise to bite our tongues in these circumstances and feel good about the fact that in doing so we will ultimately get the sale and we will have beaten the prospect at his own game—we'll be able to feel superior, if we want.

Other messages get our egos embroiled in the selling process. *Control* is one of them. Some people have driving personalities. They want to be in charge of all situations and feel ill at ease when somebody else has the reins.

These kinds of people try to control the selling and buying process by setting the agenda early in the conversation and by earmarking what they are really interested in right away. When you deal with these kinds of people, give them control. Don't battle over who will lead the sale to a successful conclusion because the prospect will take care of everything if given the control he or she has indicated. Resist the prospect, and you'll probably find you end up having an argument rather than getting the order. Another message that gets us ego-involved is *strategy*. Clients sometimes ask us a series of questions without revealing what they are leading up to. We should not get uptight if we find we're in the middle of a session of twenty-questions. You might ask the person, "What are you really looking for, may I ask? Perhaps I can save you some time."

Evaluation is a defense-producing message that we should avoid at all costs. For instance, when customers call us to complain about the widget we sold them that won't work, we should avoid giving them the feeling that *they* are a problem and that they are being personally evaluated for the breakdown. An evaluative message would be: "You shouldn't have opened the seal on the case. That's where you really blew it." An alternative to this would be probing for the information we want. "Is the seal on the case broken? I see. This is probably where the problem came from." The latter statement says the same thing but tends to avoid giving the client the feeling that we are punishing him or her with an unspoken aspersion like, "You bozo!"

Certainty is a message that I should personally avoid using, and it seems as if I am probably inclined to use this one more than any other because I am a consultant. Organizations hire my firm and myself to determine what their problems are and how to get rid of them. Because I work with a large number of companies, I have developed a substantial data base on what seems to work in certain situations and what doesn't. When I see something that I've seen before, I'm inclined to say, "What we have to do here is this . . ." This suggestion indicates to the client that there is only one way to solve a problem, which isn't necessarily true. By seeming *certain*, you can stifle innovation and challenge others to prove you wrong, which is a waste of valuable time and energy.

Neutrality can cause problems, too. This is an "I don't really care" attitude that can get into our sales transactions if we don't watch out. Clients can take up a lot of time without deciding to buy, and we can react negatively with the attitude, "Look, it doesn't matter to me whether you buy or not." People tend to resent neutrality, and they'll often try to get a rise out of us to snap us out of our pose of indifference.

FIGHTING WORDS

Nonsalespeople as well as experienced ones use language that invites interruptions and resistance. Believe it or not, the words in question aren't severe, harsh, or profane, as you might expect. They are quite the opposite. They are *overly polite*.

Look at the following sentences. The first sentence contains certain phrasing that we might call "very polite." The second alters this in some subtle, yet significant ways.

1. "So, what I'd like to do is come over tomorrow afternoon and discuss this proposal with you."
2. "So, what I'll do is come over tomorrow afternoon and discuss this proposal with you."

Did you sense the difference? The first phrase *asks permission* of the prospect with the words, "like to." This is really just another way of asking, "May I come over tomorrow?" If we put our request in this manner, we'd be unlikely to get the number of approvals that we'd get by using the second approach.

The second line is much more *assumptive*. Here, we aren't asking if we can stop by, *we're telling them what we're going to do*. By telling, we create substantial momentum that someone will have to get directly in our path to stop, which isn't too likely.

You're probably telling yourself, "I don't like this technique. It's too aggressive for me." I agree that this could seem a little harsh if we allow our voices to sound too serious as we speak. What we need to do is give our voices a light quality as we utter assumptive words.

Imagine you are telling the prospect, "You've just won a million bucks!" Now, how would you break that piece of news? With seriousness in the voice, or with exuberance and lightness? You'd probably let your voice go, and the tone might be lighter than you are used to using in most situations. This is precisely the same sort of feeling that should be in the voice as we say assumptive things.

"What I'd *like* to do," is just one of a number of "devil terms" that get in the way of selling and cause the prospect to argue with us. Watch out for other permission-asking words, such as "can I," and "you might consider," and wishy-washy terms such as these. What they do is make your prospects have to make a decision, which can cause uncertainty and nervousness on their part. Don't force people to make difficult decisions if you can make them on their behalf with much less screaming and kicking.

THE MAGIC OF TRANSITION PHRASES

I have an aunt who has a very unique communication style. I asked her about it a few years ago, and she shared some of her patented methods with me. One of her charmers is: "If somebody asks you a question you really don't want to answer, make believe that you haven't heard it in the first place." I've tried this, and it really works beautifully in social situations with family and friends. I don't think it would work too well with people we are trying to sell.

Prospects expect us to respond to their objections and questions, and if we choose to ignore them, they tend to get very angry. There are times to answer objections, though, and other times when we'll want to acknowledge them, but not really answer them.

A very good way of responding to interruptions and objections is through the use of *transition phrases*. These phrases serve to bridge from the difficulty back to smooth terrain. Here's how they work. Let's say your client tells you, "I'm not interested" at the very beginning of your sales talk? Where do you go from there?

You could fight with the person by challenging him or her: "Why aren't you interested?" This wouldn't help your cause very much. Another alternative is to try to answer the objection at that point in the talk. This doesn't succeed because you still sound like you are sparring with the prospect. The reasonable thing to do here is to *agree with the person and continue your talk as if nothing of great significance had been said*.

Assume the prospect says, "I'm not interested." What do we say? We can use any one of the following transition phrases and bridge back to the presentation.

1. Well, I understand that, but . . .
2. Well, I appreciate that, but . . .
3. Well, I know what you mean, though . . .
4. Well, I respect that, however . . .
5. Well, I'd be surprised if you were at this point, but . . .
6. Well, I recognize that, but . . .
7. Well, I agree with that, but . . .

What does this do? It acknowledges the interruption and allows us to continue in our appeal in the hope that we will strike a chord and arouse the person's interest as we move through the talk. I remember selling a particular person some years ago after she had impatiently told me she wasn't interested as I announced my name. I quickly shot back at her, "Well, I'd be surprised if you were at this point, but . . ." and she laughed and remained silent until I finished my talk. The next thing I heard from her was "okay" when I asked for approval of the order.

We should be warned against using too many transition phrases with the same customer. Sometimes, you'll find that you need them to control the conversation, and you might enlist the help of two or three. If it seems to you that you are contending with a barrage of early objections, you will probably be better off letting the prospect go and looking for a more receptive one.

Transition phrases should be said in the same pleasant tone of voice that you were using before you were interrupted. This will assure you that your tone won't be inadvertently making it seem to customers that you are arguing with them. Properly used, transition phrases sound pleasant and even respectful. They are indispensible tools in managing resistance.

THERE IS A TIME TO COMPLETELY ANSWER OBJECTIONS

After hearing about transition phrases, you may have been wondering if we would ever deal with objections directly. We do, however there is a time to answer objections and a time to simply acknowledge them.

Here is the guideline.

A. If you are *not* at the point in your talk where you are asking for approval or closing, use transition phrases to bridge back to the presentation.
B. If you *are* at the close, and you are given an objection, answer it to the best of your ability, and close again.

These are important principles. If you answer an objection without attaching a line to close to it, you will be forcing customers to close themselves, which they are unlikely to do. Furthermore, there is situational power conferred upon you when you immediately ask for approval after successfully defeating a challenge. You are saying, in effect, "Now that I have overcome your hurdle, there is nothing standing in the way of approving this sale, right?" If your prospect hurls another negative at you, follow the same procedure: Answer the objection, and immediately close again. The results should be dramatic.

THE BASIC OBJECTIONS

There are certain basic objections that we encounter across selling situations. Pleasantly, there are some basic answers available with which to deal with them, also.

No Money

You'll hear this objection phrased in various ways—"I can't afford it," is a common variant. People use this line as a stall or as an excuse when they really do have money, but something else is standing in their way. There are a number of approaches to dealing with this one.

"It's only pennies a day . . ." This is a translation made for clients who see only the initial price and nothing else. By breaking down the awesome total into the actual life of the product, we can "prove" that the investment is really very reasonable. Dishwashing liquids advertised on TV do this very effectively.

"You get what you pay for . . ." This is a common belief in our culture. We've all had the unpleasant experience of buying second-rate goods that fall apart quickly, and end up costing us more than the "good stuff" would have.

"Don't think of this as an expense, but as an investment . . ." It helps our cause if we can make an expensive item appear to pay back its purchasing price over a short period of time.

"Fine, we'll just send you half . . ." This is very successful if you are dealing with a commodity that can be broken down into smaller units. It also serves as an instant-close method.

"We're not for everybody . . ." This is a snob appeal that says we're expensive and we're proud of it! Before thinking that this would boomerang, check your clothes closet. Do you own any designer jeans that have somebody's name stitched on the back? This sort of fashion, more than anything else, tells the world, "Look, I'm one of the special people who can waste his or her money on a status symbol."

I have often heard premium retailers respond to accusations that they are too expensive with the positive words: "Well, it's true that we are the Cadillac of our industry." The obvious implication is: "Are you a Cadillac person?"

No Time

People use this objection as an excuse very often. They'll say, "I'm really busy," and most salespeople put their tails between their hind legs and waddle off into the sunset. I encourage salespeople to say: "So am I, so I'll make this brief."

That's right! So are *you*. Your time is valuable too. Remember that and be proud of it. You're important and busy, as well, and if you weren't, people wouldn't want to talk with you because you'd probably appear to be "just another nerd."

As with transition phrases, you voice needs to remain calm, and you need to say it very quickly, yet gently. Now, practice this line: "So am I." Doesn't it feel good?

No Interest

Would you be interested in something you never heard about before? Of course not. That's why salespeople exist, to create interest and desire where little or none existed before.

Don't be surprised when you hear this objection as "I'm not interested." As mentioned before, use transition phrases to bridge back to your talk if the interruption comes before you have arrived at the close.

If you hear this at the end of your talk, where you have already given the prospect the benefits of the product or service, try to clarify the person's goals with a qualifying question that really puts the matter right in front of them: "As I understand it, you *are* interested in making some serious money on a small investment, aren't you?"

This will do one of three things.

1. The person will agree. You can then say that your plan will do precisely that, and then proceed to close.
2. The person will disagree. Say good-bye, because you probably are dealing with a zombie.
3. The person will reveal his or her *real* objection that was being masked by the phrase, "I'm not interested."
   From this point, all you should do is answer the revealed objection and close again.

No Need

When you hear that somebody thinks he or she doesn't need something, it is time to do some serious probing. Ask a number of direct questions to establish the need. If this doesn't do it, you are probably dealing with somebody who isn't being straight with you. If you agree with the person that he or she really doesn't need what you have, go on to the next prospect as soon as possible.

We Use Your Competitor

Few people are 100 percent happy with their suppliers. Even if a supplier has the greatest products and staff in the world, buyers still wonder if they can't get the goods just a little bit more cheaply. When you hear someone say they are dealing with the competition, you have a few options.

1. Ask the prospects what they like most about the competition, and what they would change about them if they could. Be prepared to hear things you don't care to hear, but they'll be valuable to you in selling similar prospects.

   When they indicate ways that would improve the competition, note them, and if you can say your firm does what the competition doesn't do, you may get a deal.

   Remember this rule of business etiquette: "They're good, but we're a little better." This is the way you should characterize the competition. Don't directly criticize them, if you can avoid it, because this will reflect poorly upon yourself.

2. If you know the weaknesses of your competition as you begin a sales transaction, you can exploit the competition by directing questions to your prospects that reveal these drawbacks. For instance, you may ask: "Have they resolved the service problems that we've heard so much about?" Or, you can ask questions about the competitor, and then "innocently" ask your prospect if these things are important to them.

3. Another general answer to this objection is to say: "Well, they're a fine company, of course, but a number of their former customers are now fiercely loyal to us, because of the [fill in the blank] we provide. So give us a try, and we're sure you'll be happy with us, okay?"

THERE IS AN ANSWER TO NEARLY EVERY OBJECTION!

If you use your creativity, you'll find there is an answer for nearly every objection. All you need to remember is the basic formula outlined here for handling objections successfully.

1. If the objections are uttered *before* you are ready to ask for the sale, *agree* with them through a transition phrase and return to your appeal where you left off.
2. If the objections come at or after you have closed, *agree* with them, *answer* them as completely as you can, and then *close again*.

Let's take "I want to think it over" as an objection and handle it as outlined. We might respond by saying one of the two following statements.

1. "Well, I appreciate that Mr. Smith, however . . ."
2. "Time is of the essence, and we may not be able to fulfill your request if you delay. So, let's reserve your [fill-in] today, and we're sure you'll be happy with it, okay?"

Let's try an absurd example. Imagine the customer says he or she only buys on Tuesdays, and you are speaking to him or her on Thursday.

1. "I respect that Mr. Frisbee, but . . ."
2. "Opportunity knocks on different days of the week, and we need to be prepared when it happens along, so we'll set aside a widget for you today, and we're sure you'll be pleased we did, okay?"

Remember, an objection isn't truly answered until you have attached a line to close to it asking for the approval of the customer.

STAYING POSITIVE IN THE FACE OF DIFFICULTIES

Salespeople are special, as you know from having read the profile of successful salespeople in a prior chapter. They need to cultivate a special ability for keeping cool under fire that many of the rest of us are never called upon to develop.

In its way, selling is like a battle. We need to stay sharp all the time and watch out for fatigue that can diminish our desire and motivation. I have found eleven tips that keep my spirits high and help me to overcome those periods of self-doubt and uncertainty that afflict all achievers from time to time.

1. Remember the Law of Large Numbers

The Law of Large Numbers may be the eighth wonder of the world. Don't let yourself get down because one or a few prospects are giving you a rough time. Develop more prospects and you'll find that the few troublesome become terribly insignificant by comparison. Keep doing things by the numbers, and I'm sure you'll find you get your share of the goodies.

2. Compose Yourself Before Every Sales Presentation

I like to take deep breaths before I am about to begin a sales talk. I think this is a holdover from my baseball playing days when we used to relieve the tension of tough situations through deep breathing.

Try to concentrate on the mechanics of selling in order to overcome any fright you may have. Think about the sequence of what you will say as you prepare. This will prevent you from becoming overly conscious of your concerns about being successful. Also tell yourself "I am going to be successful," and *visualize* prospects buying from you. Put a smile on their imaginary faces, and you'll find you become much more relaxed as a result.

3. Don't Stop on Bad News

I recently spoke to a salesman who was about to quit his job because he heard two pieces of bad news in a single day. Apparently, two clients decided to cancel orders that he had worked very hard on. I told him that the best thing he could do was continue working because by producing new sales he would inevitably bring up his attitude. Quitting would only make things worse for him.

When my attitude gets negative, I instruct myself to do *something* constructive right away, no matter how minor. This means that I may feel terrible, but I'll insist that I accomplish perhaps 10 percent of a goal that I had set forth for myself. Additionally, I tell myself, "Anything I do will be a miracle, because I feel so lousy, so get in there Goodman and at least have a good time."

What does this do for me? It loosens me up considerably. I no longer feel that I have to be perfect. In fact, in telling myself that it's okay to do poorly I find the opposite occurs. I relax, and I find that I accomplish a great deal very quickly in this mood. As a result, I decide to plow forward and accomplish a lot more than the original 10 percent I told myself to do.

4. Try to Sound Customer-Oriented

I discovered a great Mexican restaurant the other night. The waiter we had was terrific, and the food was unique and tasty. I was especially impressed by the waiter because he noticed that we were new customers, and he took it upon himself to explain a number of specialties of the house.

He treated us as well as any other table and we gave him a nice tip, which was well deserved. A few nights later, we returned, and there was another waiter who took care of us. We noted that he became much chillier toward us when he discovered we weren't having alcoholic drinks, which tend to escalate the tab and the tip. He doted on people who were drinking and practically ignored us. Our waiter was not *customer-oriented*, as he should have been. We could tell that he was really out for himself and that we were there to help him to make a living, and that's all.

It's easy to recoil unto ourselves as salespeople and perceive that "it's us against them," and that customers are only "scores" who provide us with a living, but are to be otherwise scorned. When we start communicating our bitterness to customers, our business usually falls apart soon thereafter. When you receive negative feedback from customers, ask yourself, "What else can I do to be of service?" Get better, not more distant to the people who will ultimately reward your efforts.

5. Close Early

When you sell, you are investing your time with people and you need to make sure that your investment is worthwhile. To the extent possible, go for an early approval of the proposition as this will not only help you to turn more deals, but it will help you to reduce your time commitment to those who aren't serious about buying in the first place.

6. Close Often

Anyone who is worth pitching is worth pursuing beyond the first objection. Set your sights upon the closing process from the very beginning of the sale, and make sure everything you say and do moves you to a close.

7. Don't Worry About Your Percentages

I have run across a number of salespeople who boast about the *proportion* of prospects they close. This number can be a misleading statistic because someone may get one out of two people to consent to a sale when he or she is only making presentations to very few people to begin with.

For instance, the person who makes ten presentations per day and closes, on the average, 25 percent of them, or (2.5) sales per day, is doing a lot better for him- or herself and the company than is the person who is making six presentations and closing 33 percent or two sales per day.

Another problem that besets salespeople is *perfectionism*. We tend to develop unrealistic expectations of ourselves when we concentrate on the proportion of sales made rather than the total number over a given period of time. In the interest of appearing infalliable, we keep ourselves from taking risks in seeing different types of prospects who are more likely, in the beginning, to say no to us than our old standbys. Keep plugging away and remember that the only thing that's really worth counting is the total number of orders you get.

8. Avoid Believing in Myths

Numbers of salespeople are superstitious and believe that forces beyond their control are responsible for the reward they reap from their efforts. I don't believe this. We cause our own results to happen, and we make our own luck.

One popular myth is, "It's not my day." People who say this make it appear that each day is predetermined in advance and they have nothing to do with the outcomes that occur. Baloney!

Another myth is, "They're tough out there, today." What does this mean? Have all of the planet's customers decided together that they were going to give particular salespeople a rough time? It may seem like it, but it really isn't so.

The problem with endorsing myths is that we can miss tremendous opportunities because we are too busy making generalizations about how things are "out there." Remember, on any particular day in various industries, records are being broken and new levels of achievement are being established.

9. Change Your Personal Routine

If you find you are in a sales slump, and nothing seems to be going right for you, I suggest you change your perspective on matters by doing something new. Get out of your rut by waking up at four o'clock in the morning and fixing yourself breakfast or a cup of coffee. Read the paper in a different room. Take a new path to the office. Smile at someone who shoots terrible looks at you. In other words, shake up your routine a bit. Start exercising, or if you already exercise, add something new to keep you interested. If you do these kinds of things, I guarantee that your day will be different. You'll also probably sell more because you'll have a jump on the rest of the world. You will become wide awake while they are still in lotusland.

10. Count Your Blessings

Corny as it may sound, I don't think I take enough time out of the day to consider the many gifts and opportunities that I have been endowed with in this life. Because I do a great deal of public speaking, I am particularly sensitive to my voice, which I have lost to laryngitis on a few critical occasions. When I found I couldn't express myself with my voice, I felt lost and my world was suddenly insecure. I shuddered at the thought that this could become a permanent condition, and that my career and entire approach to life would require radical alteration.

When I feel that the world is giving me a rough time and I begin to rebel, I try to stop myself and think of the basic human abilities that I take for granted. This reminds me that I have a responsibility to make the most out of each day and to be thankful that I have an opportunity to flourish through selling my products and services.

11. Make Someone Laugh

One of the best ways I have found of elevating my mood is by making someone else laugh. When I see the other person laughing, I start to laugh too, and things look rosier right away.

It doesn't matter where you are, either. I once rolled down my window as I was leaving a car wash and motioned to a driver who was entering the lot. He stopped, rolled down his window, and I told him a joke. I don't know what he enjoyed more—the joke or the oddball situation that I chose in order to tell it.

Objections are an inseparable part of selling, but we don't have to be defeated by them or discouraged either. By preparing ourselves to handle them as they come along, we'll feel more secure and find that we enjoy selling that much more.

We're now going to turn our attention to a tool that can save time and energy as well as help us to become much more productive—the telephone.

chapter six

Professional telemarketing techniques

Imagine being able to stay in the comfort of your own office, in all kinds of weather, conduct more business than you ever have, and accomplish this without seeing a single customer. Does this sound too good to be true? Impossible?

Well, it isn't. People who develop *telemarketing* skills find that they can actually be more productive, in many cases, than they have been in the past by using the telephone as their number one customer contact tool.

The amazing thing is that people in all industries are now starting to "Reach Out & Sell Someone,"™ because they find that customers are quite receptive to doing business through this medium, while it saves sales costs for the sponsoring organization.

The typical cost of an industrial sales visit is set between $160 and $300. This means that each and every time a salesperson gets into an automobile or airplane to visit a client, the "meter is running" and a goodly sum is being spent, *irrespective of whether a customer buys*. The phone can cut costs to a tenth of what they are through wise planning and use.

WHAT CAN AND CAN'T BE SOLD BY TELEPHONE

My firm, Goodman Communications Corporation, has pioneered telemarketing and management seminars throughout the United States and one comment we used to hear was, "You can't sell such and such by tele-

119

phone. You have to go out and *see* the people." Over the years we have come to doubt this claim so much that I believe "You Can Sell *Anything By Telephone.*"TM In fact, this is the title of a forthcoming book that I am presently writing.

Do I mean that you can sell fine art by telephone? Yes, and our company has developed methods for doing so. Can we sell angry customers a new product when they have called us to complain about another product they have bought from us? Absolutely, if the conversation is managed professionally. Can you sell large ticket items, such as intangible investments? Yes, again. Some of our clients sell investments priced at $10,000 to people on a single cold call, where they have never had prior contact with the customer.

Typically, the phone has been viewed as a poor substitute for a face-to-face contact, or as an appointment-setting device only. We have one client in the air cargo industry that used to conduct its telemarketing efforts with this limitation in mind. The only thing reps were able to do was set appointments for field salespeople, and if prospects weren't shipping enough to warrant a personal visit, they couldn't do business with the firm unless the prospect initiated the contact.

We changed all of this by challenging the basic assumption that cargo services, themselves, couldn't be sold by phone. We trained the national telephone force and provided them with a systematic approach for handling 95 percent of the contingencies that they would encounter on the phone. Within 90 days, the firm found its shipments, which had been averaging 20 per month, shot up to over 500 per month, with no net change in their manpower.

The key to helping this firm to be successful was in convincing them that much more than they ever thought could be accomplished by phone. This thought, by itself, can start people along the right path.

THERE'S MORE TO IT THAN MEETS THE EYE—LITERALLY

When we first start using the phone for selling, we often find we are working with a much more complex medium than we thought. Because we no longer have eye contact with the prospect, it is much more difficult to monitor how our message is doing through the visual feedback customers provide through facial expressions and body language.

There is a certain amount of vocal body language apparent in phone conversations that sophisticated sellers become aware of and use for their benefit. After you use the phone for awhile you'll develop a sixth sense for the reactions of the customer. For instance, your listening skills will probably become sharpened, and as a result you'll tend to make sense out of the sighs and other cues that buyers send to us without being conscious they are doing so.

CREATING CREDIBILITY BY PHONE

Sometimes it is easier for a customer to dismiss us and our message because we are just a disembodied voice rather than a flesh-and-blood person who is in their presence. They can also come to disbelieve or doubt our message because they "don't know who they're talking to," as telemarketers come to hear. What can we do to overcome their reservations with doing business by phone?

Building credibility by telephone is essential to success as I point out in another book of mine, *Winning by Telephone: Telephone Effectiveness for Business Professionals and Consumers* (Prentice-Hall, 1982). How can we do this?

There are three things that make us credible or believable to prospects, according to behavioral research: (1) trust; (2) expertise; and (3) dynamism. To the extent that we come across to customers as possessing these characteristics, we will seem credible to them, and if we are credible, we'll be persuasive.

CREATING TRUST

People tend to trust others who are like them, and tend to distrust those who aren't like them. This trust or distrust is caused by *identification*. Perhaps the most significant part of persuading somebody is in showing the person that we are *like them*. Can this be accomplished by phone?

The way to seem like another person on the phone is to *sound like the other person*. Just as the three-piece suit and briefcase are badges of affiliation for numbers of businesspeople around the world, the voice is our badge of affiliation over the phone. When you call a particular region of the country, such as the South, you would be wise to sound like a Southerner, and when calling the East, like an Easterner.

Change your voice in three basic ways. Alter the *rate* at which you speak, or speed up and slow down depending upon the rate at which the other person speaks. Alter the *melody* or the pitch in the voice to match the other person's, and alter the *volume* or the loudness of the voice to meet the other person's as well.

You'll find that your prospects start opening up to you more, and the defensiveness you previously felt was there when speaking with folks from a different region will diminish significantly.

You might be asking, "Isn't this phony?" [No pun intended here.] I don't think so. If you ever lived in different regions of the country, as I have, you probably found that your accent or dialect changed at least slightly as you went from place to place. This is a normal part of adjusting to our surroundings and an unconscious device we choose for getting along with others. On the phone, we ask you to let your voice change as it would if you were actually in the different regions for a substantial period of time. If you're like me, you'll find that getting along with different types of people is exhilarating and profitable.

SOUND LIKE YOU KNOW YOUR STUFF

Credible people are perceived as knowledgeable. In fact, a former university president once said, "Knowledge isn't the possession of facts, alone—it is the *organization* of those facts."

It's true, knowledgeable people are organized. This is why it's so important to plan your telephone calls so you know exactly where you are headed before you pick up the phone. Many telephone salespeople fail because they beat around the bush, repeat themselves needlessly, or "get lost" in the middle of a thought, and don't know how to extricate themselves.

When my firm develops a telemarketing program, we formulate scripts that reps are instructed to use. These are typed and are distributed to everyone so they can have a basic talk in front of them at all times, as well as answers to common objections. We have found that the best salespeople appreciate these tools and rely upon them, no matter how well they think they know the presentation. When salespeople get off of the pitch, and start to wing-it, their productivity sinks. For a number of examples of telephone sales scripts see my book, *Reach Out & Sell Someone* (Prentice-Hall, 1983).

BE DYNAMIC!

A strange transformation overcomes people when they leave face-to-face selling and get on the phones. They often inadvertantly leave their personalities behind, as well. Instead of having the p-zazz and verve that they do when they are making a personal presentation, they "flatten-out" and sound bored, and worse, boring to the customer.

Vocal exercises help us to sound more lively and dynamic on the phone, and this helps us to keep the interest of the prospect. Make sure you cultivate *vocal variety*. This means that different thoughts should sound different as you express them.

For instance, if in your sales talk you are making a transition from one concept to the next, make the ideas stand out a little bit. "This is really a rare opportunity, Mrs. Jones, and you'll find it's a much more economical way to invest your money, too." This segment expresses two different ideas. "Rare opportunity" should be said as if the speaker really means it. There might be a slight "hush" in the voice as the speaker says "rare," and when the words, "economical way," are used, the voice should sound happy and perhaps, relieved.

An occupational hazard gets in our way in sounding too expressive on the phone. Because so many presentations are made during a short period of time, our ideas can start running together, and we can sound like we're reading from a canned pitch. This tone is something that should be avoided at all costs. Even if we have heard ourselves give the same talk hundreds of times, we have to remember that it is totally new to each listener, and it needs to sound fresh and spontaneous to be successful.

Vocal variety can be practiced through the use of a tape recorder and a newspaper. Try reading the same article into the tape recorder in different ways. Select an attitude with which to tell the story. For instance, you might choose anger as your initial tone of voice, to be followed with affection. Play back the various versions you recorded and note how truly expressive your voice can be when you concentrate on making it more interesting.

COLD CALLING

Cold calling is speaking with people with whom we have had no past contact. This type of calling is referred to as the most difficult form of telephone selling, because we don't have any positive past history to rely upon in our conversation and we need to establish rapport very quickly.

Cold calling is perhaps the most effective way of starting and growing a business, because it brings in customers that we probably wouldn't otherwise get. These customers can then be used as referral sources and help us to expand further.

One of the tricks to cold calling is in allowing the Law of Large Numbers to do its work. Out of any given population of prospects, you'll find that a certain percentage, perhaps 5 percent to 25 percent, will be ready to do business with you simply because you called them at the right time. Getting to enough people with your message is essential.

KEEP CALLS SHORT

To contact a sufficient number of people, we need to keep our calls as brief and to the point as possible. This means that the typical cold call should last no more than three minutes before we ask for some sort of commitment from the prospect.

Calls should follow a four-part sequence: (1) opener; (2) description; (3) close; and (4) confirmation. The *opener* is an ice-breaker and our excuse for calling. There are several available, ranging from the inactive account approach to the referral approach to the after-mailing approach. One of the most important points to remember about the opener is that we should create a two-way conversation whenever possible. This means that you should announce who you are, the name of your company, and then ask the person how he or she is, or ask him or her to respond to a specific question. By getting the person talking, you will be getting the person involved in the call immediately, and he or she will be more likely to want to listen to the remainder of your talk.

The *description* step is where you mention 2 to 4 benefits of your product or service. Limit the number of benefits because people don't have very long attention spans when talking on the phone, and you will sound *in*credible if you rattle off too many benefits.

The most common mistake made in the description step is to make it too lengthy. A good rule of thumb is to cut it down to one-half of the length that you think it should be. Customers will be grateful, and you'll end up speaking to more people, as a result.

The *close* is important in all telephone selling, whether you are looking to actually write an order while on the phone or whether you are simply gathering information to be used later in a face-to-face follow-up with the client. Remember this rule: Accomplish as much as you can with each telephone contact. If somebody sounds interested in what you have to offer, ask them for commitment right there on the line.

I was speaking to a prospect several weeks ago, and the person expressed an interest in sponsoring one of my telephone marketing seminars at his firm. Toward the end of the call, he asked me what the next step was, and whether I should come out and see his operation. I said it wouldn't be necessary, and the next step was to set the dates for our program. He agreed, and the only time I had to see the fellow, and spend a few hours driving to his location, was when I was doing the program itself. In other words, I was able to accelerate the relationship by gaining as much commitment on that telephone call as I could. I can't tell you how much time, energy, and money I have saved over the years in following this simple rule.

Some of you may be asking yourselves, "What if I try to close prematurely. What will happen?" Probably nothing, except you will be that much closer to getting the business when you have your next opportunity to close.

I have found that the checkback close that we discussed in Chapter Four works very well in selling products by phone, and in engineering total commitment through this medium. Recall that the checkback close tells us to make an assumptive statement and checkback with the prospect for approval of our decision with words such as, "Fair enough?" or "Okay?".

SETTING APPOINTMENTS

I think that setting appointments is the easiest aspect of telemarketing because it involves little risk on the part of the prospect. All he or she is doing is setting aside a little time to speak with someone, which isn't very threatening. A super closing statement for setting appointments is: "The calendar indicates a good time for Frank to stop by will be between two and three on Thursday, or will Friday be better for you?"

You probably noticed that I used a choice-close in setting the time of the meeting. This is done because schedules are hectic, and it makes sense to give the client some choice in the matter. At the same time, I haven't asked the client to make a yes or no decision. The client isn't being asked *if* he or she would like to see Frank, but *when*. This is crucial because it assumes that it's only natural that he or she would want to see him, and now it's only a matter of agreeing on when that will be.

I also have fun in setting appointments because I use the language, "The calendar [or schedule, if you prefer this word] suggests a good time will be . . .". Why is this important phrasing? I am putting the choice as to the proper time for a meeting on the lips of the calendar instead of my own. People don't argue with Father Time or Mother Nature nearly as much as they will with Gary Goodman, so I make it sound like the date and time have been chosen by forces larger than ourselves. The words, "will be" are also strong. I avoid wishy-washy terms such as, "might be," or "should be."

You will probably come across people who use wording such as "I'm going to be in the area on Tuesday. I can stop by either in the morning or afternoon. Which will be better for you?"

I have some problems with this phraseology. First, when we tell somebody that we are going to be in the area, we are cheapening the significance of the proposed meeting with the person with whom we are speaking. "Stopping by" is so casual that the prospect may stall us and tell us to call them the next time we think we'll be there. I also believe that in making it seem to the prospect that we are making a *special* effort to see him or her, we are likely to create a sense of commitment on his or her part that can contribute to a sale.

The wording in this example is weak for a few additional reasons. The salesperson is saying that he or she "can" stop by. This weak term asks permission of the customer. "Which will be better for you," makes the alternatives of time seem equally desirable. In my first example you'll note that I stated a particular time will be good, "or will Friday be better for you?" I have loaded the deck here, and made the first option sound better than the second. This relieves the prospect from having to make too much of a decision, while it helps me to steer people into desirable openings in my schedule.

TELEPHONE COURTESY AND MANNERS

Numbers of telephone salespeople turn off customers because they are not schooled in the basics of telephone courtesy and manners. Capable telephone salespeople take care to not offend people, while still embodying the assertive characteristics that successful salespeople need.

One of the main turn-offs for customers is the salesperson who dominates the call without allowing the client to get in a word or two of his or her own. This is simply bad manners. As mentioned, we should involve the customer from the very beginning of a call.

We should also remember to be nice to secretaries and receptionists. In my monthly *Telephone Effectiveness Newsletter*, I have written an article on the impact of secretaries and receptionists upon sales. If they want, they can effectively roll out the red carpet for us when we call, or they can trip us on our way to the executive suite. Salespeople should make a point of treating these functionaries with respect and strive to develop a friendly relationship with them. It makes a big difference, I have found, when I call a company and say to the receptionist, "June, this is Gary Goodman calling for Martha, please." The simple use of a name can be very helpful to me, because she'll sense that I belong to the firm in some way, and when she tells Martha I am on the line, her voice could sound positive, which will have the unconscious effect of making Martha more receptive to my call than she might otherwise be.

Use of words such as "please" and "thank-you" are not only pleasing to hear, but they are pleasing to say, as well. When you have spoken to a prospect who has given you a really rough time, I suggest you say to the person at the end of the call, "Thank you for your time," or "Thank you for your courtesy," as if you really mean it. You'll find that the call ends on a pleasant note and that you are psychologically prepared to deal with the next contact in a more positive way.

BEWARE OF RECEPTIONISTS

Receptionists are really salespeople. They sell clients on doing business with us, or they "un-sell" them, based upon how they come across. If they are harsh and impatient, this can really have a profound effect upon profits, as one company's experience points out.

One firm that retained me found that it was losing customers in droves. I made a point of studying not only the sales and customer service departments, but also how receptionists were handling incoming calls. It turned out that the number one source of customer irritation was in getting through the switchboard, and after a certain number of unpleasant transactions with the lions at the gate, a good number of customers gave up and took their business elsewhere.

A major manufacturing firm in Toledo had a secret weapon in one of its receptionists. She had the capability of matching a voice to a name after hearing them once. According to legend, this person had a three year leave of absence and returned to the firm. She was answering the switchboard one day, and a fellow called and asked for an executive without announcing his own name. The receptionist instantly said to him, "How have you been, Mr. Smith?" He was startled because he had only spoken to her on one previous occasion, and that was years beforehand.

This receptionist was doing a great selling job because she was making customers feel important, and by the time they reached the parties with whom they wished to speak, they already felt a bond with the firm. Everyone who has customer contact is a salesperson, whether he or she is aware of it.

TELEPHONE FOLLOW-UP

The phone may be used very effectively in following up sales calls that have been made in the field and in keeping in touch with clients once they are on the books. I knew a fellow in the leasing business who made a point of speaking with all of his accounts every 30 days, and he found that he got more repeat and referral business than anyone else in the organization.

INCOMING SALES CALLS

There is a great deal made out of the presumed differences between selling customers who we call versus customers who call us. There aren't that many material changes that need to be made in our approach to one call or the other.

All calls tend to follow the four-part sequence that we discussed earlier in this chapter: the opener, description, close, and confirmation. When we handle an incoming call, the customer provides us with the opener, so all we need to do is bridge from this point to the remaining steps. We only need to select the right product to sell, describe it, gain approval, and confirm the particulars of our agreement.

UPGRADING CUSTOMER PURCHASES

If we could simply increase the amount customers order from us by 10 or 15 percent, our profitability would soar. Here's why. When we make a sales call and a client agrees to buy ten widgets, we have already invested a substantial amount of time in building a relationship with the person. If we can simply convince the person to accept twelve widgets instead of ten, it will take very little of our time at that point in the call, and the value we will realize from the bolstered order will help us to prosper.

There are a few ways of sweetening the deal and increasing the average yield from calls. When you reach your confirmation and you are simply verifying mailing addresses and minor details, mention to the customer in an offhanded manner that the widgets you are sending to him "normally come boxed 12 to the box" and it will save him or her some time and shipping expense to simply take a full box because he or she "can always use the widgets, right?"

If you are in charge of determining what goes into a box, you can do this with great ease and you'll be amazed at the results. Another way to upgrade purchases is to sell an accessory item that goes along with the main purchase in some related way. Again, you want to sound off-the-cuff with your announcement of the availability of these other items. Because the pressure of the main sale item is behind you, you'll find customers are much less resistant to agreeing to accept the additional items.

OVERCOMING PHONOPHOBIA

I have found that numbers of people are *phonophobics*—they are afraid of using the phone to sell. They are afraid, for the most part because they fear rejection and failure.

We need to put these fears into the proper perspective. Fear of rejection is a normal concern over the phone because we are going to speak to more people than we possibly could face to face, and a certain proportion will reject our offer. What we need to do is understand that rejection of our message *isn't rejection of us*.

I know a number of salespeople who use a "phone name" somewhat like actors who use a stage name. They conceal their real identity, and in doing so, they feel that the rejection they encounter isn't aimed at them but at this other identity. Therefore, it is easier for them to dissociate what they are experiencing from themselves.

Fear of failure has been driven into most of us since we were children. Many were told not to fail in school because you'd be held back and you'd be a source of shame to the family. What we weren't told is that failure is often an indispensable part of success. I am fond of reminding people that the great Babe Ruth held another record in addition to the home-run championship. He struck out, or failed, more than anyone else of his era, as well. He didn't let his failures get in the way of his success, and he must have understood that the same grand swing that catapulted balls out of the park also missed by a mile on a number of occasions. If he didn't try as hard, he wouldn't have failed as much, but he wouldn't have succeeded as often, either.

How can we overcome our phone fear? There are two basic ways. First, we shold tell ourselves before all calls, "I am going to be successful." Visualizing success will put a winning tone in our voice and our enthusiasm will be persuasive to customers. Second, you might start out with minor telephonic challenges. Simply call a list of people and ask them a series of questions. After you get used to speaking with different types of people, you'll become comfortable, and you'll be prepared to risk more by pursuing more challenging sales objectives. Over time, you'll come to see the telephone as a very effective and desirable tool.

TIE THE PHONE TO OTHER CAMPAIGNS

The telephone can increase your company's yield from advertising and direct mail marketing campaigns. By calling selected lists of recipients of appeals we can boost the ordinary response from direct mail by a factor of 10 times. Moreover, using multiple media is credible to clients.

In one campaign that we developed for a company, we highlighted the fact that "You've probably seen some of our ads on TV." I'm sure that numbers of people who responded affirmatively had not seen the ads but thought they had because they saw the ads of the competition. In any case, they felt they should have seen them, and for many folks, seeing *is* believing. If something's been on TV, it must be okay, or at least this is what we tell ourselves.

DON'T WORRY ABOUT CALLING PEOPLE TOO OFTEN

People who are new to telemarketing entertain the naive belief that if we have called somebody once, we can never call the person again with an offer because they will get upset or will remember our first appeal so vividly as to diminish our impact.

Clearly, this isn't valid. If you alter your "reason for calling" in the opener, you can call people every four to six weeks without causing them to feel negative about your product or service. When we are dealing with a limited universe of prospects, it is necessary to make sure we are getting the most from our calling lists. Frequent calls assure us that we are exploiting the potential of our client population.

Remember something else, too. You might call a company today, and next week the person with whom you spoke could be working for somebody else. His or her replacement may be much more highly inclined to do business with you. If you fail to stay in touch, you won't realize the benefit of the changing of the guard.

I recall working with a sales rep who was calling a list of prospects and he happened along a person who became quite irate. The fellow said, "Don't you ever call me again. I don't need what you're selling."

The sales rep was so surprised by the person's strong reaction that he got up from his desk and mentioned the call to me. I told him not to let it throw him off the track and that he should get back on the phone right away, which he did.

The very next day the rep told me a fascinating tale about the same customer. Apparently, because he was so shaken by the prospect's reaction, the rep forgot to cross off the person's name from his calling list. When he started calling the next day, he mistakenly called the fellow who had reacted so negatively the previous day.

The rep was in the middle of his sales pitch before he realized that he was speaking to the guy who had been so much trouble, so he went through the entire presentation as well as he could. To his amazement, the fellow agreed to the proposal without any hesitation. We figured that the buyer was reacting to something other than the sales message the day before, and he used the call as a means of striking out at someone, even if it was the rep who had nothing to do with his real problem.

GETTING PROFESSIONAL HELP

The typical organization that gets into telemarketing experiences some immediate success. It finds that sales costs are reduced and productivity increases. Unfortunately, this initial success goes to the heads of people in the firm, who believe that they have come to know everything that is pertinent through seat of the pants wisdom.

Most companies don't come close to exploiting the potential of their telemarketing programs. Sometimes the reason is political. There are entrenched interests in firms that don't want to see a telemarketing unit succeed because it may threaten the power of an existing traditional outside sales team. Companies also waste a lot of time trying to graft interpersonal selling methods onto a telemarketing program. As we have discovered in this chapter, telemarketing requires new skills of adjustment on the part of salespeople. They have to deal with voices alone, and train their own to be highly expressive.

Companies also make several mistakes in terms of hiring, training, motivating, and compensating reps. The typical person who will do well in outside sales may do very poorly in inside selling. Training programs that emphasize product knowledge tend to fail because we invest too much money with reps who may not have the telephone skills required to do an effective job. As a result, we end up with a very knowledgeable person who is a burden instead of an asset, and we shuffle the person off to another department in which he or she doesn't really belong.

While these subjects are covered in detail in my book, *Reach Out &* Sell *Someone*, it is important to note that the telephone is a powerful selling medium that should be used as much as possible in the most sophisticated ways. I suggest companies that are getting into telemarketing attend seminars in the field and consider hiring consultants to review their procedures from time to time, and develop new ones where appropriate. The most progressive organizations *do* argue with success, when they can exploit even more effective techniques and avenues of profit.

Afterward

Thank you for reading this book. I hope it will give you a new perspective on the selling process, and make you feel more comfortable and confident.

I love to learn, as you probably do. One of the ways I grow as a professional is by receiving feedback from people who attend my sales seminars across the country, as well as read my books and *Telephone Effectiveness Newsletter* and listen to our cassette training libraries.

I would like to hear from you if you have any questions about selling that my firm may assist you with, or if you would like to share any experiences that you think will be helpful to others who might encounter similar circumstances.

Please address any correspondence to:

Dr. Gary S. Goodman
President
Goodman Communications Corporation
P.O. Box 9733
Glendale, CA 91206

Or call us at (213) 243-7338.
Best wishes for your continuing success.

Index

Accents, regional, 40
America, as selling society, 24–25
  and salespeople, 24
  status, problems with, 24
Anger, 104
Appointments, asking for. *See* Telephone, marketing through
Articles, writing of, 41
Assumptiveness:
  power of, 37–38
    inevitability, semantics of, 37
    and salespeople, 37, 38
    self-preparation, 37, 38
    and sales strategy, 107, 108
Assurance, extra step for, 94–95

Bad news, dealing with , 115
Bartlett's Familiar Quotations, 57
Benefits, pointing out of, 92–93
  and gains, 93
Blunt language, 104

Calls. *See* Telephone marketing
Certainty, effects, 106–107
Chamberlain, Richard, 58
Clients, as goodwill ambassadors, 94–96

referrals, 96
testimonials, 95
Clippings, 41
Closes:
  assumptive, 94
  checkback, 94
  choice, 93
  early, 116
  often, 116
  trial, 95
Colleges, 20
Comfort, of prospects, 45–46
  involvement of, 45
  self-persuasion, 45
Communication of Innovations, 71
Competence, 32–35
  appearance, 32
  body language, 34–35
  numbers, use, 33–34
  power, projection of, 35
  and sales interview, control of, 32–33
  self-confidence, 34
Competition, getting jump on, 112–13
  their weaknesses, 113
  your advantages, 113
Compliments, 43
Composure, 38, 39, 114–115

Conscious vs. unconscious, 2
Constructive actions, as therapy, 115
Control, by clients, 106
Courtesy, in phrases, 42–43
  commands, 42
  polite words, 42
  requests, 42
  thank-you notes, 43
  updating of clients, 43
Credibility:
  accessories, 29
  appearance, 27–28
  cars, 27–28, 30
  clothes, 28, 29
  facelifts, 28
  hairstyles, 28
  and humility, 30–31
  jewelry, 29
  makeup, 28
  and similarity of salespeople to buyer, 27
  suits, 27
  uniforms, 29
Customers, matrix of:
  affiliation style, amount of independence, 76–77
  clothing, 74–75
    convenient, 74
    fashionable, 74
    traditional, 74
    women, 74
  deliberation, style, 75–76
    decisive, 75
    indecisive, 75
    moderate, 75
    tests, 75–76
  discussion, 69
  energy, 69
  environment, 73–74
  innovativeness, 71–73
    early adopters, 71–72
    laggards, 72
    mainstreamers, 72
    signs, 72
  intelligence, 70
  matrix, use of, 78, 79, 80
  outlook, 70–71
  perceptual style, 77–78
  personalities, rational vs. intuitive, 78
  scoring, 79
Customers, orientation to, 115–16. See also Credibility; Telephone, marketing through

Davis, Betty, 7
Decisions, individuals' reactions to, 3
Disinterest, 104

Edison, Thomas, 9, 10
Ego involvement, 105, 106, 107

Employees, as salespeople, 20–21
  and customer service reps, 20
  and self-resale of customer, 21
Entrepreneurs, 22, 23
Esquire, 12, 13
Evaluation, by clients, 106
Excess politeness, effects, 107

Failure, fear of, 9–10. See also Self-confidence;
    Success, alphabet of
  persistence, 10
  and warnings to children, 9
Fear, 104
Fischbeck, Dr. George, 35
Forbes, 57
Future failure, fear of, 10

Girard, Joe, 27
Goodwill, 41
Greetings, power of, 38
Growth, personal, 23–24

Hidden talents, 23, 24
Hill, Napoleon, 57
Hopkins, Tom, 59

Ignoring, of questions, 108
Inactive accounts, 96
Interest:
  arousal of, 112
  and defensiveness, 105
  and genuineness of, 105

Jackson, Stonewall, 66
James, William, 57

King, Alexander, 8

Laughter, use of, 118
Law of Large Numbers, 8, 114
Lewis, Jerry, 26
Lincoln, Abraham, 10
Lombardi, Vince, 58

Money, myths about:
  aphorisms, 11
  phone, sales on, 12
  self-limits, 12
  and success, myth about, 12
Money, objections about, 110–11
  costs vs. benefits, 111
  snob appeal, 111
Morita, Akio, 76
Multistage selling, 96
Myths, about selling:
  abrasiveness, 4–5
  avoidance of, 117

canned pitch, 4
compulsive liars, 3–4
diversion of attention, 5
enthusiasm, 5–6
personal burdens, 6
and professionals, smoothness of, 4
restaurant, example, 4
self-liberation, 5
straight commission, 6

Need:
establishing of, 112
identification of, 92
Negative selling, 89–90
Neutrality, 107
Newsletters, use, 40–41
Nonprofit selling, 19–20

Objections:
answering of, 110
unusual, meeting of, 113–14
One-stage selling, 96
Openers, 90–92
list, 91
specific, 90
Order-taker vs. order-maker, counterpersons as, 21–22

Peak performance, obstacles to, 12–13
Peale, Norman Vincent, 57
P.E.P. format, 35–36
Percentages, calm about, 116, 117
Perfectionism, 8–9, 116, 117
case, 8, 9
Permission-asking words, 108
Persistence, 10, 50, *See also* Success, alphabet of
Personal space, 43–45
author, experience of, 44–45
desks, 44
markers, 44
radius of, 44
Personal Space: The Behavioral Basis of Design, 74
Politics, 20
Projects, getting support for, 22
Prospects, qualifying of, 96
Purchase, motivation for:
accomplishment, 81–82
beauty, 82
consistency, 86–87
convenience, 86
equity, 82–83
excitement, 87–88
freedom, 83
friendship, 85–86
happiness, 83

importance, feelings of, 88–89
inclusion, 87
knowledge, 89
love, 84
needs, 81
peace and tranquility, 82
pleasure, 84
prosperity, 81
recognition, 85
security, 83
self-respect, 84–85
self-rewards, 88
understanding, 86

Reach Out & Sell Someone, **123, 133**
Red Cross, 19, 20
Rejection, fear of, 7–8
false belief, 7
fear of, 7
and Law of Large Numbers, 8
points to remember, 7–8
Resistance to selling:
arguing, 100–01
as challenge, 99
consumer self-protection, 101–02
80-20 rules, 100
as percentage game, 100
personality problems, 102–03
power, reasons for resistance, 101
product, problems with, 103
as test of salesperson, 102
unrelated problems, 103
Rogers, 71
Roosevelt, Franklin, 14
Routine, personal change of, 117
Ruth, Babe, 10, 130

Sales:
asking for, 49
clubs, 41
universality of, 25
visits, costs, 119
Salespeople:
image of in America, 2–3
training, 2
Sandwich technique, 39
"Scarcity sells" rule, 55
Schuller, Robert, 57, 82
Secondary-gain trap, 13–14
brochures, as excuse, 14
friendship, nature of, 13
nature, 13
Self, Robert, 85
Self, as greatest asset, 23
Self-confidence, lack of, 14–15
action as tonic, 15
exercises for meeting fears, 15

Self-confidence, lack of *(cont.)*
  and performers, 15
  and sales trainees, 15
Self-esteem, building of, 15–17
  defeat messages, 16
  downers, dealing with, 16, 17
  success messages, 16
Selling, nontraditional, 17–19
  costumes, 18
  gadgets, 17, 18
  waiters, 18, 19
Shoemaker, 71
Showdown, selling as, 1–2
Smith, William A., 41
Solution, announcing of, 92
Sommer, Robert A., 74
Strategy, of clients, 106
Success, alphabet of, 48–67
Success, fear of, 10
Superiority, feelings of in clients, 105–106

Telephone Effectiveness Newsletter, **127, 134**
Telephone, marketing through:
  accents, 122
  appointments, setting of, 126–127
    asking permission, 126–27
    choice-close, 126
    effort in, 126
    language in, 126, 127
  body language, 121
  bonuses, 129
  calls:
    confirmation, 125
    description, 125
    opener, 124–25
  cargo services, case, 120
  cold calling, 124
  credibility, creating of, 121
  and eye contact, 120–21
  followup, 128–29
  frequency of calls, 131–32
  incoming sales calls, 129
  involvement of customer, 127
  names, 127

  and other campaigns, 131
  organization of facts, 122, 123
  others, identification with, 121
  phone names, 130
  phonophobia, 130–31
  professional help, 132–33
  programs for, problems with, 132, 133
  and promotions in firms called, 131
  range of sales, 119–20
  reactions to calls, drastic changes in, 131–32
  reasons for calls, 131
  receptionists, 127, 128
    effects, 128
  rejection, fear of, 130
  rejection, of offer vs. self, 130
  scripts, 122
  secretaries, 127
  spontaneity in, 123
  upgrading of purchases, 129–30
  voice:
    control of, 121
    success tone, 130, 131
    variety, 123
Time, limits on, 111
Transition phrases, 108–10
  bridging back to presentation, 109
  reasons for use, 109
  use, 109–10
Trust:
  building of, 31
  and self, revealing of, 31

Voice: *see also* Telephone, marketing through
  clarity, 39
  loudness, 38, 39
  softness, 39
  tones, 38

Winning language, 23
Winning By Telephone, 121
Women, 28, 74
Worthington, Cal, 60

Ziglar, Zig, 48, 57